Looking at Churches

A professional photographer with a lifelong interest in churches reviews England's architectural treasures in parish churches up and down the country, indicating special points of interest that casual visitors might overlook. He provides brief histories of buildings and styles from Saxon to modern times, making this a guide that will enrich the pleasure of everyone who stops in town and village to 'have a look at the church'.

Widen Your Horizons with this new series

Remember that we cater for all interests. See for yourself with our expanding list of titles.

Places to see

Leisure activities

Sporting

Holidays

Forthcoming titles

Looking at Churches

David Bowen

David & Charles
Newton Abbot London
North Pomfret (VT) Vancouver

ISBN 0 7153 7011 1
Library of Congress Catalog Card Number 76–8622

Set in 11 on 13 Bembo
and printed in Great Britain
by Redwood Burn Limited, Trowbridge and Esher
for David & Charles (Publishers) Limited
Brunel House   Newton Abbot   Devon

Published in the United States of America
by David & Charles Inc
North Pomfret   Vermont 05053   USA

Published in Canada
by Douglas David & Charles Limited
1875 Welch Street   North Vancouver   BC

Contents

Introduction

When we look at a church we are looking at living history – a tradition dating back over the centuries for us to examine and admire. Every church has a fascinating human story to tell. Nor do our churches merely represent the building of a few years; most of them have continued to grow and evolve, faithfully reflecting the changing values of the centuries.

Some people are put off visiting churches because they consider themselves 'not religious' and feel it somehow wrong to go inside. But churches are for individuals to sit and think in, as well as for the worship of congregations. Above all they are places which welcome any visitor, as they have done in England for over fourteen hundred years.

Roman Beginnings

Sadly, none of the very first churches built in England have survived, but it is important to remember what sort of places they were. They appeared when Britain was still a province of the Roman Empire, and they served its people until their final defeat.

Under the Roman Empire, Christianity had to survive the vicious cycle of persecution and toleration before it became the official religion of the Empire. To start with there were no churches; early Christians had to meet informally, usually in private rooms. A major change came after centuries of endurance in 312, when the Emperor Constantine was converted to Christianity; and in the following year the Edict of Milan allowed Christians full scope to practise their religion. Permanent places of worship now sprang up throughout the Empire. They were closely modelled on the *basilica*, the Roman court of justice and civil administration, and the name (meaning 'house of the king') survived to signify 'church'. The simple plan of the basilica, with a *narthex* or porch at the west end and the nave leading worshippers to the altar at the east end, became the basis for church design through the succeeding centuries.

After Rome fell in 410, Roman Britain was left to its own devices. The decaying province fought gallantly against the relentless waves of pagan Saxon invaders, but the latter triumphed in the end and effectively drove Christianity out of conquered 'England', as the island began to be known. When Augustine and his fellow missionaries from Rome restored Christianity to the southern English in 597, the king of Kent gave them an old and ruined Roman church, St Martin's in Canterbury, long ago vanished, in which to worship. This building would have been modelled on the basilica plan, which lived on in the churches built by the Christian kings and people of Saxon England.

1 Saxon (*c.* 600–1066)

Background

The oldest churches found in Britain today date from the Saxon period (*c.* 600–1066). At first only larger towns and settlements had churches. The countryside was primitive and villages mere encampments. Services were conducted in the open at special meeting places in or near villages. These places were marked by commemorative crosses, many of them beautifully carved. Later, the crosses were covered by thatched canopies, and eventually similar shelter was provided for the worshippers. Most early parish churches evolved in this way, in contrast to the more formal designs built in Kent where Roman influences from the Continent were naturally strongest.

Landowners gradually took on the responsibility of building their own wooden field churches to serve their estates; they appointed their own priests, known as secular clergy (the beginning of lay patronage), who came under the spiritual authority of the bishop. Clergy were paid partly by voluntary offerings and partly from the small amount of land – the *glebe* – granted to them. Dues were later paid from tithes. In time field churches were enlarged or rebuilt to serve surrounding areas or parishes. Some new churches were built by monastic orders.

New waves of invaders swept down from Denmark in the middle ninth century. Towns, villages and churches were destroyed. But Wessex, England's southern kingdom, was the least affected and it became relatively more powerful, providing the foundation for a kingdom of all England. The Danes eventually accepted Christianity. During the stabilising reign of Alfred the Great (871–901), church and state affairs became well integrated. Kings made laws for the protection and upkeep of churches, while clergy assisted in the administration of civil laws.

From late Saxon times churches were used as courts of justice as well as for religious services. The bishop, the supreme ruler within his province – later called a diocese – exercised authority over monastic houses. In large provinces the bishop would delegate some of his powers to subordinate clergy in outlying 'minsters' or churches. The familiar Saxon word 'minster' originally stood for a 'church of the monastery'.

Saxon church laws had always been very strict. For example, King Ina of Wessex (688–726) imposed fines upon parents who failed to baptise their infants and on those who laboured on Sundays. Dwellings were valued at Christmas, and the rate imposed upon their owners, called church-shot or light-shot, was payable on the following Martinmas.

Some 1,700 churches were built between the fifth century and the Norman Conquest, but few survive intact. Bradford-on-Avon (Wiltshire) has an almost unaltered Saxon church. Between 100–200 Saxon churches have been partly preserved by being incorporated in later buildings.

Saxon and the later Norman churches are collectively known as *Romanesque*, meaning 'after the Roman manner'; but for the many Saxon churches that were crudely built in wood or stone in the Celtic tradition this description is misleading. Most of the later, more advanced Saxon churches are found in the Midlands limestone belt. These are larger than their predecessors and have high architectural merit.

Saxon Style
Simplicity is the keynote in all Saxon work. Those churches that follow the Roman basilica pattern have a round chancel, known as an

Two-celled Saxon church, with apsidal chancel separated from the nave by an arch

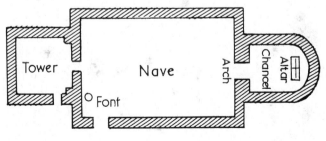

9

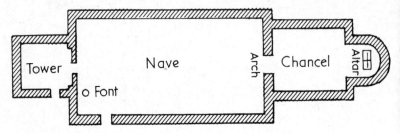

Three-celled Saxon church: nave, chancel, and altar sanctuary. The east end is still apsidal

apse, that is slightly narrower than the nave – the open area where the congregation worshipped – and a fairly large porch at the west end, which was the equivalent of the old Roman *narthex*; they may also have (or originally have been built with) small chapels on either side of the junction between the nave and the apse. From the Saxon period onwards chancels always appear on the east side of the church.

Saxon apses are either semi-circular or polygonal, but most churches did not have apses and were planned with a rectangular east end. This soon became the normal English style.

Typical Plans of Saxon Churches
Two-celled: nave and sanctuary, separated by chancel arch. Nave rectangular; chancel apsidal or rectangular. *Example*: Escomb (Co Durham).

Three-celled: nave, chancel, and separate sanctuary at east end. Nave and chancel normally separated by an arch. Nave rectangular, chancel apsidal or rectangular.

Four-celled: or five-celled in cruciform shape. Similar to above style, with the addition of one or two *transept* arms – extensions projecting outwards from north or south (or both) sides. *Examples*: Breamore (Hampshire); Bradford-on-Avon (Wiltshire). Saxon transepts are generally short and well defined. *Example*: Worth (Sussex).

All Saints, Brixworth (Northamptonshire) is an unusual Saxon Church. Of monastic origin, it was damaged during Danish raids in the late eighth or early ninth century and rebuilt in the eleventh century. Its aisles are formed from pillared arcades of Roman bricks. Part of the narthex at the west end survives, integrated with the tower.

Aisles

Original Saxon aisles are rare. *Examples*: Wing (Buckinghamshire); Great Paxton (Huntingdonshire).

Walls

The earliest timber-framed churches had walls of wattle and daub panels. In the only surviving wooden church, at Greensted (Essex), part of the nave walls incorporate some original Saxon oak timbers. This church owes its survival to various renovations over the centuries.

Walls of Saxon stone-built churches are 2–3½ft thick; early walls were built with large, roughly squared stone blocks, strongly mortared. Corners (*quoins*) were generally strengthened with very large stones, or, in the case of fine late churches, with alternating vertical and horizontal slabs known as 'long and short work'. Here upright stones are rectangular, 2–4ft in height, while the horizontal stones butt into the wall and may project slightly. Plaster was used to cover walls, inside and out.

Ornamentation was sometimes used, and the interlacing rope pattern is typical of this. Chevron (zig-zag) patterns appear in some late work. *Examples*: tower interior, St Benet (Cambridge); sides or *jambstones* of windows at Wansford (Northamptonshire).

Saxon exterior walls at their finest feature thin rectangular *pilaster strips* set vertically into the mortar. This imitates timberwork, and is not structural.

Wall arcades (arched thin pillars attached to the wall) were sometimes used, as were horizontal string courses of stone showing the division between storeys – of a tower for example. These project slightly and are also purely decorative.

Quarrying and transporting stone was difficult in Saxon times. Stoneless districts made use of Roman bricks and other material.

Towers

Towers for churches were a Saxon innovation, popular and practical. They were used for bell ringing, and as look-outs in coastal regions. Windows are usually high set, and few. In the east, towers are generally round, built from flints and pebbles to save importing squared quoin stones. Otherwise Saxon towers are square, with no ledges; they are found on the west side of the church, with an entrance to the nave through a small round archway.

Central towers are rare. *Example*: St Mary, Breamore (Hampshire). Masons of the Saxon era had not yet mastered the later art of building towers on piers, connected by arches.

Saxon church towers can be quite high, up to 70ft or more. They were roofed with low caps covered with suitable local material, including thatch. The only original tower roof is at Sompting (Sussex). This lovely *helm-spire* shows Rhineland influence.

Belfries were a usual feature, but no original bells remain from the period. Belfry openings are narrow with a dividing baluster-shaft, carved like wood, resting on a solid through-stone. The usual alternative is a bellcote, built under the west gable of the nave wall.

Late Saxon towers are highly decorated, with round or triangular windows and thin pilaster strips. Towers were sometimes built over the west porch with the second storey serving as the priest's dwelling – a custom later forbidden. Internal windows to the nave allowed the priest to recite the midnight offices in full view of the altar, without leaving his tower. *Examples*: St Mary, Deerhurst (Gloucestershire); Brixworth (Northamptonshire).

Roofs

Supported by roughly hewn timber trusses, Saxon church roofs featured external boards or rafters covered in lead, tile or thatch. Thatch or turf was usual on early wattle and daub churches. No original Saxon nave roofs remain.

Pillars

Saxon pillars are simple, dignified, and round, often tapered towards the top and roughly hewn from large blocks of stone. A typical decoration is an interlaced or spiral carving. The top of pillar or *capital*, which supports the arch above, is round or lozenge-shaped; the *base* has a similar shape but is smaller and splayed. Some late capitals are sculptured, with various designs and images.

Arches

Saxon arches were formed by wedged-shaped stones. They were normally placed between the nave and the chancel, except in Cornwall, parts of Devon, and in the Craven area of Yorkshire. Saxon arches also appear above the pillars of aisled naves and in the few vaulted crypts. Many arches are sculptured.

Doorways

These are round or triangular-headed, or with flat lintels. Where the doorhead is round, it is formed by wedged-shaped stones resting upon crudely-carved capitals and jambs.

Windows

Also round (often with a dividing baluster-shaft) or triangular-headed, with the jambs converging slightly. The earliest Saxon windows were cut through wall with little or no splay, flush with the outer face; later they were splayed on the inner side to enlarge the opening. Very late work may show a double splay, the outer being generally the slighter of the two. Triangular heads and double splays are exclusively Saxon. Circular openings were occasionally used in the transitional (Saxon–Norman) period.

   To keep out draughts openings would be filled in with oiled linen, but sometimes wooden shutters were used. Deeply splayed windows could be left unfilled or unshuttered.

Porches

Of Roman basilican or monastic origin, Saxon porches normally have an opening on each face. At Brixworth (Northamptonshire), and Monkwearmouth (Co Durham), the porch forms the lower storey of a tower. Bishopstone (Sussex), has a south porch. Both transept arms

Twin, round-headed Saxon windows high in the chancel wall at Wing (Bucks)

at Bradford-on-Avon (Wiltshire), originally contained porches.

Altars

No original Saxon altars remain. The earliest were simple wooden tables representing that used at the Last Supper, known as 'Christ's Board' or 'God's Board'. A law of 750 ruled that altars should be made of stone. They were about 1ft thick, 10ft in length, and were touched at each corner and in the centre with holy oil at consecration, to symbolise the five wounds of Christ. These places were later marked by incised crosses.

Fonts

Deep stone tubs, some with sculptured decoration, placed just above floor level. Baptismal candidates stood in the font, and water was poured over them. Deerhurst (Gloucestershire) claims to have the finest and best preserved Saxon font.

Piscina

Early examples are very rare. Used from the ninth century onwards for rinsing sacred vessels and the hands of the priest celebrating the Mass, the piscina is a stone basin built into the wall south of the altar, which drains into consecrated ground outside the church.

Paintings and Sculpture

Figures in relief were painted in a variety of colours. The sculpture on internal stonework is usually of Celtic or Byzantine origin, with portrayals of Christ (including Crucifixion scenes), saints, apostles, and angels. There were also animals and symbolic representations.

Sculpture appears on *roods* (crosses), arches, pillars and capitals, fonts, and grave-slabs. Hampshire has six sculptured roods, Bradford-on-Avon two prostrate figures of angels high on the chancel wall. Wall roods and *tympana* (semi-circular stone fillings beneath arches) are found at Romsey Abbey (Hampshire), and Daglingworth (Gloucestershire). Other items include an early sundial at Marsh Baldon (Oxfordshire); a frieze, Breedon-on-the-Hill (Leicestershire); a coffin lid, Wirksworth (Derbyshire); and a series of buttress carvings outside the chancel, Fletton (Huntingdonshire).

Furnishings

Coloured hangings were used in Saxon churches. Floors were normally plain – stone slabs around the chancel, otherwise pressed earth covered in rushes for warmth. There were no seats at all.

Music

Choral singing in plainsong, also known as Gregorian chanting, was a monastic tradition that spread to parish churches. It was developed by Pope Gregory the Great on the older antiphonal style of western Europe, with two choirs singing in alternation. Pope Gregory set the liturgy to a complete musical setting, which St Augustine introduced into England. Harmony was not attempted until the tenth century. Organs – large in size and volume output – were installed in a few important churches; they were used for accompaniment and bear no relation to present-day instruments. Keys were operated by fists, not fingers!

Crypts

Crypts are large cellars with several compartments built under the chancel of larger churches and cathedrals, and are rare in churches of any period. They were used for storing valuables, including sacred vessels and books, and later (at cathedrals) for enshrining relics. *Examples*: Brixworth (Northamptonshire); Repton (Derbyshire); Wing (Buckinghamshire).

Crypt roofs were normally supported by stone vaulting. Wing (Buckinghamshire) originally had wooden beams, later replaced by a simple barrel-shaped vault. An inner wall around the crypt encloses a circular passage or *ambulatory*. The principles of vaulting had been mastered by the Romans, but were not applied to the spanning of large sections of roof in England until after the Norman conquest.

Stone Crosses

These marked places where Christians first worshipped, and represent the first visible signs of post-Roman Christianity. Once they were numerous, particularly where good stone was available. Examples in various states of preservation, but often showing fine workmanship, can be found in Northumberland, Cumbria, Yorkshire, Derbyshire and Lincolnshire, through Gloucester to Cornwall.

Crosses are of Celtic origin and were sculptured in relief in the typical patterns of the time. Animals and human figures are often represented. The shafts are tall and incorporate a wheel-shaped design backed by a carving of Mary and her child. Sometimes there is a second smaller cross carved in relief about half-way down the shaft. At Ampney Crucis (Gloucestershire), and Sowerby (Lincolnshire), the crosses are complete.

2 Norman (1066–c. 1200)

Background

Fierce energy, military might, and strong continental influences characterised the Normans, originally a gang of Norsemen who carved out a homeland for themselves at the expense of the northern French. Their conquest of England after 1066 had profound effects on the thinking of the English church, the new men who ran it, and the fabric of its buildings.

The harsh new Norman era was the first great age of church building in England. At first few parish churches were built as the emphasis was on large buildings – monasteries and cathedrals. But the long-term Norman plan was to give every village a permanent stone church. Few original Saxon churches had survived, as most had been built of wood. The Norman practice was to enlarge older buildings where possible, and local English craftsmen acquired many new skills from the master masons brought in from the continent.

The North was the exception: it had been singled out for savage punishment after the great revolt by the northern English in 1070–2, and all previous Saxon churches and dwellings were ravaged to make the North a desert.

In 1154 the Norman line of kings gave place to the Plantagenet line of Henry II, but the Norman style of building continued until near the end of the century. By then fine new monasteries and parish churches had been built in all parts of the land, and the parochial system had been greatly strengthened.

Norman Style

The Norman church is powerfully built, with very thick walls, generally small round-headed windows, and short, squat towers. Walls, arches, and windows are often richly carved.

Typical Plans

Two-celled (smaller churches); separate nave and chancel – longer,

Norman strength: the round nave of the Church of the Holy Sepulchre, Cambridge

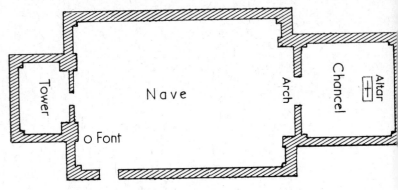

Two-celled Norman church, with nave and rectangular chancel

somewhat wider than the Saxon — separated by a round-headed arch. Nave rectangular; chancel rectangular or apsidal. The apse was discontinued after a time owing to extra cost of construction and the problem of shaping stones in the round. It also tended to restrict space.

Three-celled (larger churches); nave, chancel, and separate sanctuary — sometimes apsidal but generally rectangular — at the end. Interiors were larger; occasionally there is a central tower above the chancel, supported by large, stone piers.

Five-celled, cruciform, comprising three cells and central tower, as above, but with the addition of north and south transept arms. *Fine example*: Old Shoreham (Sussex).

Circular; built by returning Crusader knights in late period, based on the example of Jerusalem. Five of these remain: Church of the Holy Sepulchre (Cambridge); St Sepulchre (Northampton); Temple Church (London); parish church of Little Maplestead (Essex); chapel of Ludlow Castle (Shropshire).

Aisles

These were added to give extra space for altars, processions, and other demands of increasing ritual. Some larger churches had aisles from the beginning. An early example is that of Melbourne (Derbyshire).

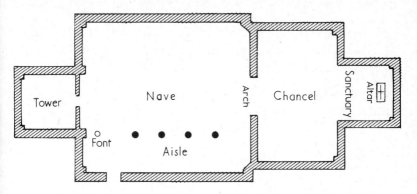

Expansion. A three-celled twelfth-century church with a south aisle added

Walls

Norman walls feature ashlar (cut stone), very thick to support heavy weight, but in two skins with inner core of rubble and mortar – a very economical use of material, to cut down cost. The herring-bone design indicates early work. Jointing was improved and narrowed in the century, but plainness or otherwise of exterior walls is no reliable guide to date.

Important churches were adorned with various types of decoration. Wall arcades are typical; lines of thinly carved arched pillars built into a main wall of a tower, or appearing round a building at various levels to make a rich embroidery. *Example*: the round so-called 'Norman tower' of Christchurch Priory (Hampshire).

Another form of decoration with structural purpose was the rectangular wall projection, wide in area but of no great depth, resembling a flat buttress.

Small blocks of stone projecting from walls at eaves level – *corbels* – give extra support to those parts of the upper surface where thrust from an interior wooden roof is greatest. Each is humorously carved in the form of a head of man or beast, or in some abstract shape. A large number of corbels at eaves level is described as a *corbel table*.

Towers and Turrets

Norman towers are short, sturdy, and normally square, built one storey above the ridge of the roof. Round East Anglian towers were preserved, with addition of a new belfry course. Hales and Haddiscoe (Norfolk) are examples.

West towers are normal, but a minority were placed above chancel, giving a cruciform façade. Some important churches have two towers at the west end. St Edmund, Bury (Cambridgeshire), completed in 1095, was built with one central and two octagonal west towers. Towers are covered with 'saddleback' or pyramid designs, on a wooden framework, and tiled. Saddleback towers are rare. Examples: Sarratt (Hertfordshire), and Elm (Somerset). Pyramid towers were usual, but most were later replaced by flat roofs and given parapets. From the small Norman pyramid came the inspiration for the great spires of the thirteenth century and after.

Abbey churches have numerous turrets, each with its cone-shaped roof covering.

Roofs

Generally made of timber trusses, with tie beams at the lowest part stretching horizontally between the two main walls. Support to the structure was given by a vertical king post or two smaller queen posts. Jointing was dowelled, for nails – apart from the type used on door hinges – had not been invented. Roofs were steep and covered with available material: generally lead, tiles or thatch.

Vaults

Stone vaulted roofs were used to a limited extent; they were uncommon in smaller churches. The first type, continuing from the Saxon period, was the barrel vault formed by round arches, supported on both sides by very strong walls: between the arches a tunnel ceiling was formed, composed of rubble and mortar.

Two barrel arches intersecting at right angles produced a groined vault, and the Norman builders adapted this Roman invention to their own requirements. The thrust to the ground is from four points – groins – where the edges of the barrels meet. Each unit was produced within the space of a square, called a compartment, and the whole solid mass was held up by elaborate wooden supports known as centering.

The groined vault, like the simpler barrel vault, had its limitations.

It was costly, unduly heavy, not particularly strong, and was unsuitable for spanning high, wide naves in larger churches. It was used for roofing aisles. *Examples*: St Bartholomew, Smithfield (London); the lower aisles of St John's Chapel, Tower of London; and the crypt of St Mary, Lastingham (North Yorkshire).

One way to strengthen a groined vault was to construct large transverse arches on two opposite sides of a compartment, but a new technique was needed before vaulting could be developed to a really useful extent. The advance came with the introduction of the *arched rib* – which proved to be much stronger than groins – and by erecting the ribs first and then filling in the triangular divisions between them. These were the *vault cells*. Less wooden centering was required, and this could be moved along as work progressed.

Norman ribbed vaulting can be seen at Romsey Abbey (Hampshire) and at Durham Cathedral, which was completed as early as 1133. It was not used in parish churches until the thirteenth century, and then only when expense permitted. *Example*: St Mary, Hemel Hempstead (Hertfordshire).

No vaulting was weatherproof; it required a normal tiled or leaded wooden roof to be placed over it.

Ribbed vaulting solved a number of problems, but created others. It was difficult to vault adjoining areas if these were of different shape: for example, a nave and an aisle. Secondly, while round arches were in use, it was necessary to raise some pillars above the height of neighbouring ones in order to span certain compartments. The process was no longer necessary after the discovery of the more flexible pointed arch.

Pillars

A *pillar* or *pier* supports an arch and comprises a *base*, *shaft* and *capital* (or *cap*) at the top. Most Norman shafts are cylindrical, plain or carved, with diagonal pattern or other ornaments of the period. In later work shafts may be compound or clustered, the latter being formed by a number of thin shafts banded together. In section the shafts are of simple squares or rounds. The larger shafts are faced with ashlar, the inner part filled with rubble or mortar.

Norman ribbed vaulting: the chancel of St Mary, Hemel Hempstead (Herts)

Norman bases are splayed squares, or square at the lowest point and moulded at the top around the circumference of the shaft. A feature of the latter type is the tongue-like carved leaf or head that softens the square into the round (or, occasionally, the octagon) of the shaft above it.

Norman caps are large and imposing. When shafts are large, the *abacus* – the upper section of the cap – is generally square. The top of the middle part of the cap is on the same plane as the abacus, but the lower part is worked into a round by creating a *cushion*. On large compound pillars this may be broken up so as to match each section of the shaft. The lower part of the cap is the neck moulding, which is just a thin band.

The cushion cap is featured throughout the whole of the Norman period and it is one of its best known characteristics. Later caps are similar in their basic form but are boldly sculptured with foliage, figures of men, beasts, or monsters. Some caps have deeply cut scallops, also known as *volutes*, at the corners.

Arches

Some are plain, others lavishly decorated. All are larger than the Saxon, but the individual stones of which they are comprised are smaller. Door and chancel arches are often compound on one side, where they are made of overlapping recessed rings – *orders* – each supported by its own pair of vertical shafts and ornately carved to contrast with the adjoining one. Early work was done with an axe; later, sharper work with a chisel. Many orders were used towards the end of the period, with striking results, and arches of south doors were occasionally selected for special treatment.

Common patterns of decoration are the beakhead, billet, cable, chequer, chevron (zig-zag), diamond, double-cone, nailhead, pellet, and star. Other designs include the *scollop*, a basket-like moulding, or, as at St Cuthbert, Fishlake (West Yorkshire) carvings composed of individual plaques of animals. Beneath the arch of a Norman doorway one may find a semi-circular stone filling, the *tympanum*, strongly carved with a Biblical scene or designs with angels in combat with dragons.

Classic zig-zag pattern and recessed 'orders' on a late Norman doorway:
St Anthony, St Anthony-in-Roseland (Cornwall)

Triforium and Clerestory

Three-storey constructions on either side of main aisles were built in principal churches. The lowest and largest section is formed by a line of pillars facing nave or chancel (or both), with arches between each to make an arcade. Above is a second, smaller arcade, which, again may be free-standing (or termed 'blind', or 'blank', if attached to the wall) at the height of the aisle roof. Known as the *triforium*, this is slightly set back to allow for an upper passage; it was used as a stage from which to hang tapestries and other decorations on festival days.

Above the triforium, set back to the outer main wall, is the third storey. This is the 'clear-storey' or *clerestory*. It is pierced by windows along its whole length and is an important source of light in a large church. Three-storey construction died out in the fourteenth century, but up to the fifteenth century many churches needing extra light had clerestories added to them at the second-storey level.

Doors and Doorways

Little Norman woodwork remains. Doors were made of oaken boards reinforced with wrought iron, with hinges fastened by large nails with projecting heads, as also in later centuries. *Examples of Norman ironwork on doors*: Great Hormead (Hertfordshire); Skipworth (East Yorkshire); and Stillingfleet (East Yorkshire). Hinges at Stillingfleet incorporate Viking ships and dragons. Later hinges were more conventional in treatment, with boldly interlacing circles.

Many old Norman (and later) doorways have been blocked up but are revealed by subsequent additions or repairs.

Windows

Round-headed, generally only of modest size but larger than the Saxon. Deep splaying is usual, to let in maximum light but keep out the weather. Sides (jambs) are straight. Beneath the window arch is a single light, or one may find two lights separated by a vertical shaft – a feature copied from the Saxons. Then came the triple window, as at Romsey (Hampshire).

Occasionally a window is treated like a doorway, with several orders to the arch, as at St Mary the Virgin, Iffley (Oxfordshire).

Norman arcade and triforium (with an Early English clerestory above) in the
nave of Priory Church, Christchurch (Hants)

Here the west front features a centrally placed round window. When carved with spokes, this type is known as a wheel or 'St Catherine' window. That at St Nicholas, Barfrestone (Kent) has eight well-defined spokes.

By the early twelfth century windows were introduced and were filled with glass mosaic between thin strips of lead. Early glass has a beautiful deep colour, red and blue predominating, and because no cutting instruments were available it is always uneven and thick.

Porches

The entrance to a parish church was from the south side, which faced the entrance path and was closest to the village. Enclosed porches of the period are rare.

Altars

Few Norman altars remain. A law of 1076 ruled that altars should be constructed of stone. One overlooked by the later reformers and discovered in its original position in Arundel (Sussex), was preserved because it had a covering of wood. The top, with the customary five incised crosses, was made as a stone shelf splayed on the lower edge like the abacus of an early pillar cap.

Fonts

Many Norman fonts have survived. The earliest, like the Saxon, were tub-shaped, as at Hartland (North Devon). On later ones the bowl is supported by one or more pillars on a large square base. As fonts became larger, bowls – normally round or octagonal – decreased in size. Later still the design of the font was square and featured one large central shaft and four smaller shafts at the corners; these were massively built and richly carved with figure subjects and other designs.

Seating

Occasionally stone seats were provided around the walls for the use of the old or infirm.

Preaching

In the days before the introduction of the pulpit, the bishop or priest would address the congregation from the chancel steps.

Floor Decoration, Paintings and Heraldry

No floor tiles have survived that can definitely be said to belong to the Norman period.

Remember, when visiting old churches, that from the earliest times to the Reformation the interiors of parish churches were made highly colourful. Pictures painted on walls gave a 'magic lantern' effect and instructed the congregation; many were of high artistic merit. *Examples of twelfth century paintings*: the apostles in the disused church at Kempley (Gloucestershire); Christ in glory, in the apse, Copford (Essex); New Testament scenes at Brook (Kent); a painting discovered in 1880 at Patcham (Sussex); and paintings showing scenes from the life of Our Lord and of St George, at Hardham (Sussex).

Kings and nobles assumed distinctive marks for their shields, and their arms were exhibited on hangings used in the decoration of churches at festivals, as also in later times.

Chests

Early chests of the period were known as 'dug-outs' and were scooped out from large logs. Warwickshire, a county famous for its oaks, has examples such as the one at Curdworth.

Bells

Used in church towers, as before, but no bells of the period have been found.

3 Early Gothic (c. 1200–c. 1375)

Background

The close of the twelfth century and the beginning of the thirteenth ushered in the 'Gothic' period in architecture. It came as a total change, and brought about the greatest era of church building in England. This was also a time when, despite many upheavals, England became a prosperous trading nation and the Christian faith became solidly implanted in the life and on the landscape of the country.

The parish church was now the natural centre of every village, and not merely for regular attendance at Mass on Sundays and saints' days. Parishioners contributed to the upkeep of the church, as today – it was their 'community centre'. The nave was used for social purposes, which included dancing, play-acting, and festive church 'ales'. Even talking during the service was not then thought of as irreverent and was tolerated except at solemn moments such as the offering of the Host.

In the increasingly prosperous fourteenth century the new wealthy classes provided money for church building and enlargement. Merchants and landowners began to pay large sums for the foundation of chantries: small chapels within a church where Mass could be said for their wellbeing or for the repose of their souls after death. Special chantry priests were appointed for the purpose; these were coveted jobs. Some churches became known as 'collegiate', showing they were attached to a college set up for the establishment of religious communities and for making rules for chantry priests.

Across this scene cut the terrible Black Death – a massive outbreak of bubonic plague – in 1348–9, which carried off about a third of the whole population. Church building was severely affected for many years, and when resumed the Gothic style moved into a different phase.

Font of early Gothic period, St Mary, Norbury (Derbyshire)

Gothic Style

Why Gothic? The term, which refers to the pointed style of architecture, was invented in the eighteenth century; it was meant to be derisory, for it was thought by the adherents of the Classical Renaissance style that anything earlier was barbaric – the allusion being made to the Goths, the warlike Teutonic race which had sacked Rome in 410. But this was grossly unjust to the soaring beauty of the Gothic style.

Gothic shows a clear break from the rounded Norman pattern, and it follows a logical sequence. 'Early English' (1200–75) is typified by the narrow pointed arch. 'Decorated', following a transitional period, lasted 1310–50 (but longer in Norfolk) and is associated with increasingly flowing patterns of window tracery.

The hallmark of Gothic is *daring*. General features include roofs of increased height and span; tall, elegant towers; soaring spires; higher nave arcades; higher, and then wider, windows; richer carving and ornament. Gone is the church's fortress aspect. Now the eyes are lifted upwards; there is a sense of mystery. And in all cases it is the *pointed arch* that makes these buildings so different from their predecessors.

Window styles give the best clues to the date of a Gothic church, though many have composite styles of architecture and decoration, having been started in one part of the period and finished in another. Older churches were also adapted to meet the new requirements. There was a need for larger buildings, with longer chancels, additional altar space, and more room for processions. This related to the greater number of priests and the more complex forms of worship, not to a sudden increase in the size of congregations.

Methods for enlarging churches varied. Transepts could be added, or, if already in existence, lengthened. Aisles, if not present, could be built on. A nave might be extended westwards (tower permitting) by building extra bays and a new gable wall. Likewise, chancels could be extended eastwards. Sometimes there were unusual problems: for example, where aisles and transepts met to form a box design.

From the fourteenth century onwards there was no definite constructional difference between nave and chancel, which were

Gothic glory: flowing Decorated window tracery, Church of the Blessed Virgin
Mary, Edington (Wilts)

often divided by a screen crowned with a cross (*rood screen*) instead of the familiar arch. The building of cruciform churches with central towers, while never universally popular, continued until the fourteenth century.

Gothic Guidelines

Early English. Narrow pointed arches and windows (*lancets*). Underpart of arch sometimes cusped or foliated. Round or clustered pillars. Pillar capitals moulded in successive chamfers or carved in heavy relief showing (normally upward-growing) foliage. Typical motif of sculptured ornament: the nailhead, also known as 'dog-tooth', which is basically a pyramid cut into a fourfold pointed leaf.

Considerable difference can be noted between large and small churches. The former may not have much ornament but always possess a simple dignified beauty.

Transitional (Early English/Decorated). Two or three lancet windows grouped together under one arch, with a geometrical pattern of small cusps or circles cut into stonework above the main lights giving symmetry to the design: this is *plate tracery*. Alternative: a composite window of simple design produced by central upright (mullion) bent at top into 'Y'-shape. On larger windows the 'Y' is repeated to form intersections.

Decorated. Pointed arch becomes wider; whole of window opening now one unified design with ribwork between panes composed of slender shafts – *bar tracery*. First style retains geometrical pattern at top of window but in larger outline than before. Later tracery shows network (*reticulated*) effect, then becomes more varied and flowing.

Patterns in carving resemble those of window tracery. *Ballflower*, a kind of circular opening bud, is the main ornament motif. Pillars wider, with more sections; capitals, if carved, show foliage (now growing horizontally) in less heavy relief. Smaller churches generally lack the richer features of period.

Early English priest's doorway at St Leonard, Flamstead (Herts)

General Features

Aisles and Clerestories

As the period developed, most new churches were designed and built with aisles. In the thirteenth century the addition of north or south aisle, or both, was the most convenient method to enlarge a church. First the aisle wall would be built parallel to and probably along the whole length of the nave, and given its own roof; next the frame and door of the old entrance was moved flush with the aisle wall; the old nave walls were then breached, one bay at a time, to be replaced by arcades. These could incorporate new pillars, or portions of the old walls were left to serve as piers. Old walling would remain above the new arcade.

In the West country and in parts of Kent aisles were often gabled and roofed in the same manner as the nave, to allow aisle windows to be the same size as the original. The same object could be achieved by a lean-to roof springing from the base of the nave roof if the latter was shallow in pitch. Where the aisle wall was much lower than that of the nave, restricting window size and light, it was common practice – except in Cornwall, Devon and parts of Kent – to build a 'clear-story' (*clerestory*). Embroidered with parapet complete with battlements and pinnacles, more of these date from the fifteenth century than earlier.

Aisle width gradually increased, later ones being seldom less than 15ft. Where churches had the normal west tower, aisles would stop short of this or be built flush against it. Sometimes aisles would be added to chancels, providing space for chapels and altars close to the sanctuary. Chancels could also have their own clerestories.

Filey (Yorkshire), Compton Bishop (Somerset), and St Margaret-at-Cliffe (Kent) have very early (and rare) clerestories of the transitional period between Norman and Early English. Thirteenth-century Early English examples are still rare: Elm (Cambridgeshire); Horsham (Sussex); Darlington (Yorkshire); Aymestry (Herefordshire). Later they became a regular feature, always displaying the latest style of windows; ultimately, the glazed area was as large as that of the stone.

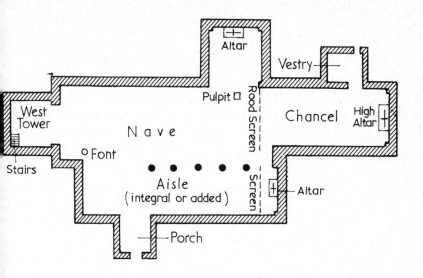

Gothic church with small north transept and south aisle, probably an adaptation of an earlier church. The rood screen is extended to provide a partition between the aisle altar and the aisle

Late Gothic church with west tower and twin aisles, providing ample space for parish priest and collegiate clergy

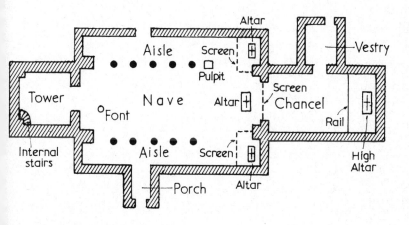

Flying buttresses, pinnacles, and crockets adorn the Abbey Church of Sherborne (Dorset)

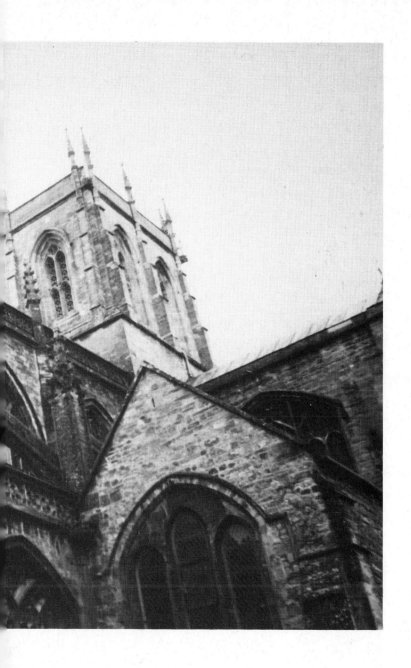

Clerestories are occasionally found in aisleless churches where aisles were no doubt intended; here they merely form a second tier of nave windows – examples: Halford and Ilmington (Warwickshire); Sandiacre and Wilne (Derbyshire). Still less usual is a second tier of windows in the aisle wall, as at Broughton (Oxfordshire).

Walls and Buttresses

Walls were now built of solid ashlar stonework or other local material, such as flint. Walls gradually became thinner, while buttresses became deeper but less wide. In the Early English period buttresses were placed two to a corner, at right angles, but a diagonal setting was normal from the beginning of the Decorated period.

Where interior roofs were vaulted *flying buttresses* – slender bow-shaped stone arches – reached from the clerestory to external buttresses rising against aisle walls; these carried the heavy roof thrust to the ground.

Aisle buttresses could be built upon foundations of considerable size and depth, and they were capped by suitably sized *pinnacles* to give them extra weight and help deflect the thrust downwards. Each pinnacle is decorated with *crockets* (small crooks on very short stems, signifying the care of the Good Shepherd) and its top piece, the *finial*.

That the walls of a church provided an ideal framework for decoration was a concept inherited by the Gothic builders from the Romanesque and brought to complete fruition. Corbels, for example, were a feature of the Early English period as well as the Norman, and were now beautifully carved.

Moulded stonework can be either plain or ornamented. The Early English 'dog-tooth' is used, either by itself or with alternating floral relief. The 'ballflower' ornament of the Decorated is sometimes used very thickly, creating a rich effect.

Towers

The tall belfry tower of the Saxon period, discontinued in the Norman, comes back into favour. Bellcotes were incorporated above the western gable of smaller village churches without towers. In one unusual case, at Preston (Gloucestershire), it was built above the chancel arch – normally the position of the *sanctus bell*, an important feature of the Middle Ages that was rung at the moment the Host was elevated.

Early English parapets are mostly plain but occasionally panelled or pierced, and towers show table courses. In the Decorated the parapets are pierced and cusped with no table courses.

Most Gothic towers have interior stone staircases, but some have lofts connected by ordinary ladders; these were roughly hewn out of oak but made to last – examples: Bishops Cleeve (Gloucestershire); and Kingsnympton (Devon). In larger churches a separate loft below the belfry housed the village armour and fire-fighting equipment.

Spires

The Gothic spire evolved from the pyramid covering of the older Romanesque tower roofs. During the thirteenth century this pyramid underwent rapid transformation. First it was heightened and chamfered at the four angles, but was still made of timber. Later came the fully developed octagonal *broach spire* with its clean pure outline. These were built in prosperous wool trade areas, such as Lincolnshire, Northamptonshire, and parts of the South and West where suitable local stone was available. The *broaches*, which are triangular-shaped masonry mouldings, support the spire base on the outside, while a series of diagonal arches support it on the inside.

In the thirteenth century, tower and spire formed a unified construction leaving neither room nor decorative need for a parapet. All spires had openings; some were built with windows which generally projected outwards and formed small gables, and each one thus formed was provided with its own distinctive arch above. Fourteenth century broach spires were often gaily decorated with crockets on the angled surfaces and window gables.

The broach was eventually discontinued. The spire base was then made smaller than the tower area, so that a parapet could be built to form a platform for carrying out repairs.

Roofs

Most parish churches continued to have roofs made of wood. The

Two-storey south porch and Early English tower at St Mary the Virgin, Churston Ferrers (Devon)

pitch became gradually less steep. The *tie-beam* construction was used in the thirteenth and fourteenth centuries, as earlier, but with more awareness of its artistic potential – and the upright sections comprising *king post* or two smaller *queen posts* were given greater emphasis and prominence.

Stone Vaults

Vaulting was rarely used in parish churches, partly because of cost but also because it was more suitable for larger buildings. All Gothic vaults are ribbed. Those of the thirteenth century show the simplest arrangement: *quadripartite* where two long (diagonal) ribs cross two short (transverse) ones to form four compartments; *sexpartite* where the ribs – now spanning two bays of an arcade instead of one – cross each other to form six compartments.

By the middle thirteenth century the *ridge vault* appeared. Its main feature is the additional long axial ridge rib which runs east to west at the highest point along the whole length. Another variation, the *tierceron vault*, has extra diagonal ribs springing from the same arches as the main ones, but instead of joining up at the principal intersections they connect with another part of the axial rib or to the central point of the transverse ribs. As additional ribs were introduced, the compartments between them became smaller and increased in number. This led to the use of a larger number of carved stone bosses, one being fixed at each intersection; panels between ribs were filled with plaster.

In the fourteenth century came the *lierne vault*, formed by addition of small decorative ribs to each panel so as to form star shapes.

Early English Pillars

Shafts are round or octagonal; occasionally a group of free-standing shafts surrounds a thin central member seen through the gaps. Where round, the diagonal flutings (grooves) of the Normans are no longer used – the whole emphasis is now vertical.

Capitals: mostly undecorated, with recessed mouldings, round or octagonal. Some are carved with generally upward-growing stiff-leafed foliage on long stalks, or perhaps human heads. Carving is deeply undercut, to show as much projection as possible.

Bases: square or octagonal in lowest part with rolls above. Often there is a hollow section – referred to as 'waterholding' – between the rolls.

Decorated Pillars

Shafts may be of simple shape, round or octagonal as in the Early English period. The more impressive are multi-shafted, with eight half-shafts, or four semi-circular half-shafts, joined to a central pier. The moulding may continue unbroken in pattern from pier to arch.

Capitals: moulded in recession when undecorated – these being more numerous than with Early English caps – and bell shaped, with deepest moulds near lowest section. When carved, the design is of very realistic foliage, with thin roll-shaped moulds above and beneath. Foliage depicts horizontal growth, generally of oak, ivy, maple, or vine, carved in sufficient relief to show light and shade but with less projections than in the Early English period.

Bases roll-shaped, in either two or three stages.

Arches

In Early English period arches are long, narrow, graceful, sharply pointed. In the Decorated period length is sacrificed in favour of comparatively greater breadth, and the point is less sharp. In the later Gothic period it is wider again, and flatter – with its outline drawn from four separate centres.

It became customary for the exterior arches of windows and doors to be shielded by a *dripstone* – a protruding upper arch and a decorative feature in its own right. In the Decorated period it took the *ogee* shape – a curve that is convex below and concave as it reaches a point at the top; later in the century an ornamented gable was usual. These shapes appear in many forms in the carving of the respective periods.

Carved porch hood of St Peter and St Paul, Northleach (Gloucs)

Doors

Much Gothic period woodwork remains, including many doors. Some are plain, generally oak, with elegant hinges. In the Early English period the scroll pattern was used. *Example*: Turvey and Eaton Bray (Bedfordshire). Thereafter patterns were formed by nailstuds, and door furniture was completed with handsome wrought-iron locks and key plates. Some doors of the late Gothic period are panelled with traceries of highly intricate design

Doors, like doorways, vary in size. Early English doors were often high, and fitted into shaped recesses that were sharply pointed and considerably higher still. Beginning in the fourteenth century, cusped stone panelling was used in the jambs of doorways as well as in other parts of the church.

Early English Windows

Tall, narrow, single lancets, splayed on both sides – deepest splay on inside – placed singly, in groups of two or three, occasionally larger groups. Pairs at Minstead (Hampshire); Carlby (Lincolnshire) and Tangmere (Sussex) – all relatively uncommon, as are larger groups: three at Boxgrove Priory (Sussex); and at Abbey Dore Abbey (Herefordshire); five at Bosham (Sussex); and seven at Ockham (Surrey). Grouped lancets, with or without a containing arch above to act as a dripstone, make a striking east window arrangement and a pleasing background to the altar.

Thirteenth-century stained glass – as at Chetwode (Buckinghamshire); Chartham and Westwell (Kent); Aldermaston (Berkshire); and Stanton Harcourt (Oxfordshire) – is now very rare. Deep reds and blues predominate. *Grisaille* glass was introduced during the period in which foliage patterns are formed by leadwork or, occasionally, by lines of colour. Early English designs portray Biblical figures within medallions, surrounded by branches of the Jesse tree or by grisaille patterns.

Transitional (Early English to Decorated) Windows

Grouped lancets under one containing arch, with solid masonry between latter and tops of lancets pierced for first time – *plate tracery* –

Early English twin lancet windows at All Saints, Minstead (Hants)

to form various shapes. These are: trefoil, quatrefoil, multifoil, lozenge, and, later, plain circles cusped on the inside. Generally only two lancets were used in this form of composition, so that the total effect was still that of a narrow window.

Y-shaped tracery was also used. This involved the use of individual stone bars (*mullions*) – hence the term *bar tracery* – and at first the mullion divided the lancet into three panes by being bent at the top into a 'Y' motif. Later larger windows with more lights were produced by intersecting mullions of this shape.

Decorated Windows

Window splays increase in size during this period, thus pushing the glass nearer to the centre of the wall. At first bar tracery was used to reproduce the previous geometrical design, allowing more space for lights in the lower and upper stages. The circles at the top are of greater diameter, and the trefoil motif, where used, is elongated into a dagger shape. Cusped wheels were also used in this section.

These designs gave way to a netlike pattern known as 'reticulated'. Here the intersections form ogee shapes. Finally there came a freer and more flowing series of designs known as *curvilinear*, where the tracery is very delicate and beautiful. Early examples retained the popular cusped wheels in the upper lights.

Yellow stain, introduced in the fourteenth century, could be painted on to both white and coloured glass. Where necessary for the design any part of a coloured pane could be scraped by a newly discovered abrasive to reveal the white below. Basic colours were still deep-toned, though red tints became somewhat lighter. In design, the medallion arrangement was replaced by a type of figurework, under canopies.

Y-shaped window tracery, Church of the Blessed Virgin Mary, Edington
(Wilts)

4 Late Gothic or 'Perpendicular' (c. 1375–c. 1509)

Perpendicular Style

When Church building was resumed after the Black Death in the middle fourteenth century, the Gothic style blossomed into its most ornate form. This was the 'Perpendicular' style, named for its soaring upright lines and tracery. It lasted from about 1375 into the beginning of the sixteenth century. The increasing wealth of the country was a key factor: in the richest sheep farming areas there would often be a spirit of rivalry between villages for the finest tower or the most impressive windows. Churches had become status symbols.

Perpendicular is an essentially English style, thought to have begun with the school of designers who built the Royal Chapel at Westminster. Gloucester Cathedral is one of the earliest examples. In Perpendicular, arches become flatter at the top; windows have upright tracery in which mullions rise vertically in most sections. The undersides of composite window arches are cusped. Patterns in the carving resemble those of window tracery, and interior wood carving increases.

Decorated motifs are much more formal, with extensive use of heraldic emblems. Perpendicular pillars are slimmer and not always capped. Most Perpendicular churches feature less interior stone carving, but where it is used it is rich. This is particularly true of exterior carving, especially around towers.

General Features

Clerestories

A general feature of the Perpendicular period. Many fine Perpendicular churches in East Anglia were built with a continuous clerestory from nave to chancel.

Towers

The Perpendicular tower parapet normally has battlements and is

Soaring beauty of the Perpendicular style – 'wafer-thin' walls and fan vaulting in the ante-chapel at King's College, Cambridge heavily decorated with pinnacles and crockets, while lower groups of pinnacles adorn the tower wall in its various stages; the whole tower may be enriched with ornaments and sculptured figures.

These grand Perpendicular towers have their accent on windows. Their many windows, with single or double openings on every storey, make them unique, for previously there were only simple openings or plain louvres in church towers. Those of Somerset, numbering sixty in all, are world renowned for their rich stone, exquisite detail and beautiful composition. Some towers have three windows abreast in the top stage (Shepton Mallet and Mendip area). Others have a continuous window area between the bell chamber and the stage below, stressing the upward sweep of the stone mullions.

Perpendicular walls often show niches containing sculptured figures and *gargoyles* (originally 'gurgoyles') – carved ends of waterspouts that gurgle as water passes through them. Gargoyles may represent evil spirits or little imps escaping from the church, which could explain why they take the form of uncanny creatures such as griffins, dragons, and other animals that have a sinister reputation. But they could also be seen as an appeal for all creatures to praise the Lord: 'dragons and all deeps, beasts and all cattle, creeping things and flying fowl'.

There are many local varieties of towers. Most are basically square in shape and topped by a *parapet* that becomes steadily more elaborate as the period progresses. Some towers are octagonal, others square up to parapet but have octagonal projection above. Typical West Country variation is the otherwise square tower that has a separate square or octagonal turret at one corner rising the full length and housing the staircase. On top it will have a small pyramid cap or *spirelet*. A local south Devon variation is the square tower with the projecting staircase midway between two corners.

Roofs

Church roof designs reached their peak in the fifteenth century. Typical of the period are the *hammerbeam* roofs of East Anglia and the *wagon* and *depressed tie-beam* roofs of the West Country. The latter are based on the original tie-beam construction but with the main base

A fine Perpendicular tower: St Mary the Virgin, Huish Episcopi (Somerset)

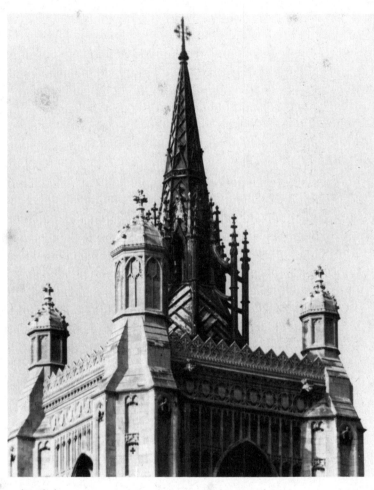

A dignified parapet spire crowns St Peter Mancroft, Norwich

A display of old roof bosses preserved at St Thomas, Lymington (Hants)

placed high and supporting a low-pitched roof.

Hammerbeam roofs, decorated on their structural parts with angels or other emblems, are so named because their supporting wall brackets are shaped like hammers. If these brackets are on two levels a double hammerbeam construction is formed. The wagon roof (its interior looking like a wagon), has a framework filled in with plaster and decorated between the intersection with *bosses* which also have a strengthening role.

Some churches favoured a plaster-filled horizontal wood panelling, as at East Dereham (Norfolk).

Sometimes the plaster infilling of such roofs was restricted to the area above the chancel, leaving the nave section open in contrast.

Wooden aisle roofs are generally of simple design, often supported by wall brackets; but even these may be carved or decorated. At St Thomas, Lymington (Hampshire), the medieval roof bosses, removed after restoration, are preserved in a special case.

Vaults

The Perpendicular style produced the beautiful *fan vault* – delicate, intricate, and certainly the most complex – of the fifteenth century. Examples: Sherborne (Dorsetshire); Cullompton (Devon); North Leigh (Oxfordshire); and King's College Chapel (Cambridge).

The panels resemble inverted cones, or fans, the tops of which are formed by semi-circular ribs joined together; thin lines of tracery within each fan complete the decorative effect. The small plaster panels between the ribs may contain ornament or heraldic emblems – as, for example, above the choir at Sherborne Abbey.

Perpendicular Pillars

Shafts

More slender, lozenge shaped or octagonal, made up of four semi-circular half-shafts with moulded fillets between them. These mouldings show much variety: wave shaped in the West Country, concave in East Anglia. As in the Decorated period, mouldings can run unbroken from the pier to the arch above.

Wood and plaster roof panelling at St Nicholas, East Dereham (Norfolk)

Capitals

Also octagonal, plain or sculptured, similar to those of the Decorated period but with deeper mouldings. Their carved patterns are more formal. Typical designs are compact foliage, angels, heraldic figures, or battlements. The uppermost of the two encircling moulds is now larger and has a slanting chamfered edge. Unsculptured capitals on complex pillars are divided into the requisite number of individual *caplets*, mounted on the shafts only and not on mouldings between them.

Bases

Shaft bases of the Perpendicular are higher than those of the Decorated period, on a comparatively high plinth. The upper section is a complex moulded feature with alternating convex and concave sections.

Perpendicular Windows

Most of the elegant but more formal Perpendicular window was made up of straight mullions. This simplified the work of the glass painter, who could insert figures of the saints in each of the main rectilinear frames. Examples are numerous, but the style reached its highest perfection in the large East Anglian and Somerset churches.

The stone tracery was structurally much tougher, for the vertical bars now rose to the top of the window; but because the trend was toward still wider windows, horizontal reinforcement bars called *transoms* were inserted between the first two stages of glass. Window arches were of the widest four-centered type, but later square frames were also used for less important windows.

Because of the Black Death there was no real transition between the Decorated and Perpendicular periods, but a few Perpendicular windows retain small sections of curved tracery in their upper parts, possibly in acknowledgement of the old tradition. *Examples*: St Mary (Warwick); Edington (Wiltshire); Curry Rivel (Somerset); Bridlington Priory (North Humberside).

Perpendicular glass is now lighter and more varied, with lovely silvery hues. A silver stain could be painted on to glass and 'fired' to produce a whole range of tints. Heraldic designs became popular.

Comparatively few medieval churches retain their original glass, but old glass is sometimes recovered, as at Fairford (Gloucestershire). In York city some churches retain their fifteenth-century glass; so do St Lawrence, Ludlow (Shropshire) and the priory church at Malvern (Worcestershire).

Some larger churches have a low side window or 'leper' window on either the north or south side of the chancel. Small bells rung here performed the same function as a Sanctus bell above the chancel, and were sounded at the appropriate moment to inform those outside of the Real Presence. The windows could not in fact have been used by lepers, who were forbidden to appear in public.

A Review of other Gothic Features

Porches

These were an important feature of the parish church throughout the Middle Ages. South porches are normal, north porches rare —

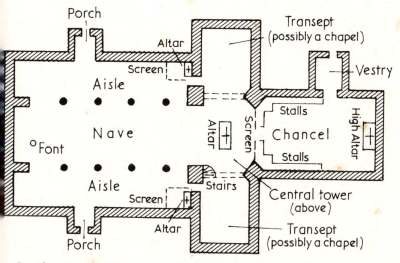

Cruciform late Gothic church (late medieval period), with permanent nave and aisle altars, twin transepts and porches, and chancel designed for use of priest and collegiate clergy likewise twin porches, as at Witney (Oxfordshire). West porches are seen occasionally. *Examples*: Broadwater and Yapton (Sussex); Boxley and Otford (Kent). Sometimes a small porch will be attached to a west tower. *Examples*: King's Sutton and Higham Ferrers (Northamptonshire). The latter has a twin entrance.

A *Galilee porch* is larger than the normal and is seen at some important churches and cathedrals. It was designed for use during the final stage of a Sunday procession at the point where the priest re-enters the church to symbolise Christ going before His disciples into Galilee after the Resurrection.

Some porches were fitted with small galleries for the use of singers as the procession entered the church. Upper chambers, sometimes called 'parvises', are more common but did not appear in any number until the fourteenth century. In the fifteenth century they were a regular feature and their outer walls were sometimes richly decorated – more so than any other exterior part. In East Anglia they were finished in *flushwork* (stone and flint) *panelling*.

Uses for the upper storey were many. Some became small chapels; others gave temporary overnight accommodation to a priest who was due to celebrate early morning Mass. They were also used by nightwatchmen. Post-Reformation uses included the housing of parish armour, books, and other items; day schools; and – as in the case of the great three-storey porch at Cirencester (Gloucestershire) – trade guild headquarters, and town hall.

Stoups

A small stone basin fixed in a wall niche, or standing on a shaft, fitted either on one side of the porch or just inside the church. When in use, it contains water blessed by the priest so that the worshipper, upon entering, may dip the fingers of his right hand into the water and make the sign of the cross as an act of self consecration.

Vestry or Sacristy

At one time the priest and his assistants robed themselves in a screened annex, either beneath the tower or in a part of the nave. In the fourteenth century many churches were built with a small rectangular addition for this purpose, which became normal practice. This is the *sacristy*, or *vestry*, having a direct access to the chancel from the north side. An external entrance was not always favoured, as the building was also used for the storage of vestments, plate, and other valuables. Sometimes a vestry would contain an altar or piscina. A few were built in two storeys. *Examples*: Chipping Norton (Oxfordshire); Raunds (Northamptonshire). Upper floors sometimes possessed *squints* through which the high altar could be seen; that at Roos (Yorkshire), has an inner window for this purpose.

Chapels

These were provided in most churches built after the middle of the period, and were set up in existing churches as required. Positions nearest to the altar were the most favoured; nave aisles and transepts would be adapted without using up all their space. Each chapel could be dedicated to a saint, martyr, or to the Virgin Mary – hence the term 'Lady Chapel'. Where size was imperative, a Lady Chapel could be built on to the easternmost side of a church, beyond the sanctuary. That at Long Melford (Suffolk) has aisles of its own and is joined to the church by a priest's house.

Chantry chapels were built for the saying of Masses on behalf of the particular benefactor during his lifetime and afterwards for the peaceful repose of his soul. Chantries increased rapidly in number in the fourteenth and fifteenth centuries with financial backing coming increasingly from trade guilds. Admission to them was restricted to the families and relatives of the individual founders or corporate guilds.

Carved wooden (*parclose*) screens divided chantry chapels from the main fabric of the church. Often the chantries would be panelled in their lower sections or crowned by magnificent arches or straight tabernacle work. Where sited close to a high altar, as at Christchurch Priory (Hampshire), they form a rich setting.

Altars and Reredoses

These continued to be made of stone up to the time of the Reformation. Most churches contained at least three altars – the principal or 'high' altar being set against the east wall of the sanctuary.

A *reredos* forms a back to the altar, and usually this took the form of a carved or painted panel. There are some fine examples of medieval stone and alabaster reredoses. *Examples*: Christchurch (Hampshire); Ottery St Mary (Devon); Drayton (Berkshire); and Elham (Kent). Thornham Parva (Suffolk), has a rare fourteenth-century wooden reredos.

There were no altar rails. The vesting of each altar was achieved by covering front and sides with a large cloth folded at the corners by individual cloths covering the same areas. It is thought that the pre-Reformation altar had only two candles, one on either side, and, in the middle, the head of the processional cross. The Blessed Sacrament was reserved in a *pyx*, but later a recessed cupboard known as an *aumbry* was more usual.

Fonts

Made of stone; originally brightly coloured. Early ones show Norman influence, with large bowls on five thick shafts, the base being square and chamfered at the edge. Then they begin to have mouldings and ornament. *Examples*: Eaton Bray, Leighton Buzzard, and Studham (Bedfordshire). Fourteenth-century fonts tended to have niches and fine carving. In the fifteenth century, the most notable period, some are on stems and decorated with panels showing groupings of evangelists, angels holding musical instruments or shields, or wild animals. At Wing (Buckinghamshire) there are projecting angels at each corner.

In the thirteenth century locked covers were ordered to prevent holy water being stolen for its supposed healing powers or other properties. At first these were simple cupboards with doors. Then came the small pyramid or bell-shaped casing lifted by a pulley. Later font covers were supreme examples of medieval carving. Norfolk has some fine carved font canopies, as at St Botolph, Trunch. The most famous of all are the *towering spire* variety. *Examples*: Ufford (Suffolk), where it is decorated with a forest of pinnacles; Balsham (Cambridgeshire); Halifax (Yorkshire).

Sedilia

Increasingly the subject of the carver's art, when the stone canopies of these in-built altar seats for the priest and his assistants were wrought in varied and intricate designs.

Piscina

Normally had two basins during Edward I's reign (1272–1307), one for rinsing sacred vessels, one for washing the celebrant's fingers before the consecration of the elements. *Examples*: Barnston (Essex); Carleton Rode (Norfolk); and Cherry Hinton, near Cambridge. One piscina, at Oare (Somerset), takes the form of a stone head. In East Anglia some were recessed into the eastern jamb of the sanctuary window nearest to altar on south side.

Stalls, Misericords, and Pews

When sermons were introduced in this period seating was gradually provided; in the choir for clergy and monks, and in the nave for the congregation. In some churches the lay patron and leading churchfolk sat in the choirstalls. In greater churches stalls in several rows had carved canopies – in parish churches one row on each side of choir, north and south, but, in larger choirs, returned sideways on either side of the chancel screen.

Choir stalls appeared from the late thirteenth century, with the beginning of tracery in carpentry. In the fourteenth century beautiful foliage carving emulated the curvilinear stonework of the period. Carving became still more elaborate in the fifteenth century, when the bishop's throne (in greater churches) would be canopied with an arch of tabernacle work.

Tip-up seats in stalls of larger churches are called *misericords*, or indulgence seats (from *misericordia*, meaning 'act of mercy'). Designed to give monks support when standing, they took the weight off their feet yet allowed them to appear upright. Elbow rests were another feature. Carvings on misericords deal widely with current life and imagery and depict historical, allegorical, hunting and domestic scenes more often than Biblical. Christchurch Priory (Hampshire) has one of the two existing contemporary portraits of Richard III.

First *pews* for the congregation were thick oak planks, roughly trimmed. *Examples*: Dunsfold (Surrey); Wensley (Yorkshire); and Skenfrith (Monmouth). Well preserved fourteenth-century pews are seen at Wiggenhall St Mary (Norfolk). Carved bench ends began in the fifteenth century, normally square-headed in the West country but often rising in impressive curved *poupée*-heads (from the French *poupée* or puppet), meaning 'figureheads'. They are also known as 'poppy-heads'. Bench end carvings are similar to those on misericords, but more often depict Biblical scenes. Some show the instruments of the Passion.

Pulpits

Placed, as now, at the south-east or north-east of nave adjacent to chancel. Stone pulpits carved similarly to fonts date from the late fourteenth century, but not many have survived. Arundel (Sussex) and Cold Ashton (Gloucestershire), have stone pulpit canopies. Wooden pulpits are more numerous. There is a fourteenth century example at Stanton (Gloucestershire). The remainder are fifteenth century, of superb workmanship, mostly octagonal, with carved panels. The most picturesque designs are those supported by central pillars, known familiarly as 'wineglass stems'. *Example*: Long Sutton (Somerset), has sixteen sides, each with a carved figure of a saint, but the actual panels are nineteenth century.

A horizontal board or canopy over a pulpit is called a *tester*. The only pre-Reformation example is in the now disused church at Edlesborough (Buckinghamshire).

Lecterns

Used for the reading of the Gospel. Most were portable, made of wood or metal, placed in the chancel. Simplest type resembled a reading desk but often had two or four sides. The more elaborate fifteenth-century type featured an eagle with outstretched wings, made of wood or brass, and incorporated three animals at the base. Only about forty old brass lecterns now exist, and about twenty wooden ones. There is an interesting wooden lectern at St Lawrence, Bigbury (Devon), a gift of Bishop Oldham of Exeter (1505–19). It was recently noticed that only the head of the lectern portrays the eagle; the bird has the body and feet of an owl.

Organ Lofts and Musical Instruments

The organ was positioned in the *rood loft* (*see below*, 'Rood Screens and Lofts') – hence the term 'organ loft'. No medieval organ case was spared in England during the sixteenth and seventeenth century puritan purges, because music was considered sinful by the most extreme 'fanaticks'. One case survives at Old Radnor in Wales. Like its Saxon and Norman predecessors, the medieval organ was primitive by modern standards. (See p 16.) Musical notation had not been invented, but the instrument provided a rough accompaniment to the singing. There was also the portative (which resembled an accordion) for use in processions, and handbells were also popular.

Rood Screens and Lofts

The *rood screen* was a highly decorative structure dividing nave from chancel. Each screen displayed a central *rood* or cross at the top, flanked on either side by statues of the Virgin Mary and St John the Evangelist. A panelled platform approached by its own staircase formed a gallery above the screen – the *rood loft*.

Rood screens reached a peak of perfection in the fifteenth century and continued to be made, without the rood, after the Reformation. Simplest screens are square-framed, comprising panels of tracery with or without ornamental overlay. More elaborate ones are arched or vaulted and crowned with canopies made up of bands of foliated carving. They are supported by a beam known as a *bressumer*. In Devon, where there is often no chancel arch, screens may run the full width of the building; the largest, over 45ft long, is at Stoke, near Hartland. Some East Anglian rood screens, also renowned, incorporate painted panels of saints. A few screens were built in stone. *Example*: Totnes (Devon). Here the mason has copied the woodcarver's technique.

The rood loft accommodated the organ, if there was one, together with the instrumentalists. It probably inspired the musician's gallery of a later period. In greater churches a more substantial fabrication,

Rood screen – restored in 1925 by Ninian Comper – and loft, with pulpit:
St Peter and St Paul, Eye (Suffolk)

the *pulpitum*, divided the choir from the nave and acted as a return for the stalls. It was solidly built, generally rectangular, carved in stone or wood.

Floors

The use of floor tiles increased. Known as 'encaustic' tiles, they were made of baked clay, normally reddish brown or yellow, but with colour variations obtainable as a result of the firing. Though made in England, they were probably of Mediterranean origin. Designs ranged from geometrical figures to human or animal heads, and armorial bearings. *Examples*: Watchet and Old Cleeve (Somerset); Haccombe, Cadeleigh and Westleigh (Devon); Launcells (Cornwall); Bredon, and Great and Little Malvern Priories (Worcestershire). Nearly complete floors have survived at Hailes (Gloucestershire), and West Hendred (Berkshire).

Brasses

Medieval brasses were made in Flanders and Germany, imported, engraved, then embedded into suitable slabs of stone or marble. The metal, known as *latten*, was hammered thin. Grooves made upon it were picked out in black or coloured enamels, though colouring has now disappeared. East Anglia and Home Counties have the greatest number of brasses: in particular, Kent, Essex and Oxfordshire.

Among fine early brasses are those of Sir John Daubernoun, at Stoke D'Abernon (Surrey), dated 1277; Sir Roger de Trumpington, at Trumpington (Cambridgeshire), dated 1289; and Sir Robert de Bures, at Acton (Suffolk), dated 1302. In early brasses the figures are deeply cut and almost life size; they wear the chain armour of the period, which was succeeded by plate armour. Fourteenth- and fifteenth-century designs included family groups, but figures were less natural in the later brasses. Sometimes clergy are shown in vestments. A number have floriated crosses.

Brass rubbing today is a very popular activity, but prior permission must always be obtained.

Effigies and Monuments

Recumbent *effigies* first appeared in the thirteenth century and are generally of excellent design. Placed near floor level, some have priestly vestments, others show armour denoting connections with the Crusades. Like brasses, they add to our knowledge of the armour and dress of the period. Details are generally faithfully reproduced.

People of note and renown would increasingly have their tombs and effigies placed within the sanctity of the church. Some had stone canopies. Many mid-period were very natural in the poses portrayed – example: Lowick (Northamptonshire), dated 1419, of a knight and his lady with hands clasped together; their heads lie on a pillow being smoothed by angels, and their favourite pet dogs are at their fet.

At this period knights received their arms from the church, which were returned after death. Effigies of knights killed in battle are clothed in armour; otherwise their arms are suspended above their effigies. Tombs were produced by local craft workshops. Nottingham became a famous centre for alabaster working in the fourteenth century. In the fifteenth century, effigies were somewhat stereotyped. Reliefs of mourners ('weepers') were carved on panelled sides of tombs; canopies became very elaborate with fan vaults and many ornamental and heraldic devices.

Easter Sepulchres

These are elaborately carved and canopied stone recesses found generally in greater churches and set into the north of the chancel close to the altar. Representing Christ's tomb, their panels of carved relief depict Roman soldiers who, though on guard, have fallen asleep. Upper panels show Resurrection scenes. *Good example*: Hawton (Nottinghamshire). At a ceremony of fast and vigil by the Easter sepulchre between Good Friday and Easter morning, the Host and altar crucifix were placed upon the tomb.

Wall Paintings

Religious life was largely guided by thoughts of Christ's passion and the need to keep to the 'straight and narrow' path to gain a place in the Heavenly Kingdom. Therefore the most prominent position for any painting – over the chancel arch – featured the great 'Doom' and adorned nearly every parish church. In it the righteous are led to Heaven by angels on the one side; on the other the sinful are tormented by demons with chains and pitchforks in Hell. At the top, Christ Triumphant awaits the arrival of the blessed. St Michael and his scales is also portrayed.

About 100 Dooms have been discovered, some having been coated by progressive layers of whitewash over the centuries. Largest Doom: St Thomas, Salisbury (Wiltshire).

Other paintings show St Christopher carrying the infant Christ across the river; the Seven Deadly Sins; the Seven Works of Mercy; Christ blessing the trades. Many date from the thirteenth century. *Examples*: St Gregory (Norwich); Dartford (Kent); Broughton (Buckinghamshire); and Breage (Cornwall).

Chests, Cupboards, Lockers, and Alms Boxes

Chests were used for storing valuables or important documents. There are few Early English examples, which are crudely made but strong; they are raised off the ground by four broad legs. Some are decorated in roundels, as on wrought-iron hinges, or bound together by iron bands. Chests from the fourteenth century and later may have carved panels and other figures. Nearly all have carefully made locks – some even have two or more for safety.

A development was the chest cupboard (*almery*, or *hutch*), fronted by two doors. *Rare example*: Louth (Lincolnshire). Later came the *dole cupboard*, an aerated box for temporary storage of bread given for the poor. *Stave lockers* for processional banners and staves are found in some medieval churches, particularly in East Anglia. Books were of great value and either chained in position or stored in a *Bible box* – interesting example of latter at Warnham (Sussex). Blythburgh (Suffolk), has an *alms box* with three traceried panels in front. Other examples at Cawston and Loddon (Norfolk), but most of these date from after the dissolution of the monasteries under Henry VIII when the number of 'deserving poor' increased, and from the seventeenth century onwards.

Consecration Crosses

When consecrated, a church would be anointed by the bishop in twelve places inside the building and twelve places outside. The former were later marked by painted crosses, the latter by small carved crosses. *Interior crosses*: Edington (Wiltshire); Holnest (Dorsetshire); Carleton Rode (Norfolk); Crosthwaite (Cumberland). *Exterior crosses*: Moorlynch (Somerset); Ottery St Mary (Devon); Uffington (Berkshire); Edington (Wiltshire).

Royal Arms

Originally painted on a square board or on canvas. After King Henry VII's reign (1485–1509), they were sometimes carved on wood, stone, or plaster, and this practice later became general.

Acoustic Jars

Earthenware jars placed below nave or chancel walls for improving

Thirteenth-century chest: St Mary, Stoke d'Abernon (Surrey)

the quality and carrying power of sound. *Examples*: Tarrant Rushton (Dorsetshire); Denford (Northamptonshire); Lyddington (Rutland).

Lighting

Services were normally conducted during daylight hours, and artificial lighting was crude. One device, the *cresset stone*, was a block of stone with scooped-out holes into which oil was poured and lit by a floating wick. Waxed rushlights could be attached to bench ends or other suitable places such as rood-beam or lectern. Thirteenth-century iron light brackets can be seen at Rowlstone (Herefordshire) and at Skenfrith (Gwent), where Early English benches have iron candle-sconces. A medieval candelabrum, formerly in Temple Church, Bristol, is now in the cathedral.

Bells

Church bells were important in medieval life and were rung to call people to worship, and for festivals, baptisms, marriages, and even for funerals – for it was unofficially believed that they would drive away evil spirits. Change ringing was not invented until the seventeenth century. Some old bells are still hanging and in regular use: they were often dedicated to various saints, and it is said but not proved that their tone was sweetened by placing coins in the molten metal when the bell was cast.

Earliest medieval bells were long and narrow. After the fifteenth century they became rounder and often carried the founder's name and a cheerful rhyme as well. Some churches retain the clappers of former bells and keep records of their history and of the ringers themselves. Ringing chambers are normally at ground level or about halfway up the tower.

Armour, Fire-fighting Equipment, etc

Among items stored in porch or tower were 'fire hooks' – which, attached to long handles, were used for cutting away smoking brushwood – shovels, armour, 'dog tongs' and other items. Fire hooks can be seen at Bere Regis (Dorsetshire). Dogs were not prevented from entering a church but were removed with whips or tongs if they entered the sanctuary.

Anchorite Cells

Piety drove some people to spend their lives in the narrow confines of a small cell built against an external church wall. The sunless northern side was often selected to achieve complete self denial. There are few authenticated remnants. Shere (Surrey) records the story of an anchorite who, having left her cell, was compelled to return to it.

5 Tudor (1509–1603)

Background

The first Tudor King of England, Henry VII (1485–1509) had been a 'medieval conservative', concentrating on healing the wounds of the long civil wars of the fifteenth century. But under his successors Henry VIII (1509–47), Edward VI (1547–53) and Elizabeth I (1558–1603), the old medieval tradition of the English Church was shattered by the *Reformation*. A brief return to Catholicism under Mary I (1553–8) could not reverse the process. The English Church broke with Rome. The monarch became its 'Supreme Head' (later 'Supreme Governor'), not the Pope. Monasteries were swept away, and so-called objects of superstition were removed from English churches, including altars and roods.

Not many new English churches were built during the sixteenth century, partly because of the religious upheaval, but also because the need for new buildings had diminished. In Elizabeth's reign, under Archbishop Parker, repairs were carried out on many churches that had suffered from neglect.

The other great sixteenth-century phenomenon was the 'Renaissance', the so-called 'rebirth' of classical Greek and Roman values in the arts. This, however, had very little influence upon English Church architecture in the period.

Tudor Style

The style was basically Perpendicular. Arches became somewhat flatter, and more square-headed windows were used. But there was no rapid transition. King's College Chapel (Cambridge), completed in 1515 but begun much earlier, displays true Perpendicular style features in its construction and possesses a beautiful fan vault. Even earlier styles of medieval vaulting were used in the early sixteenth century, as occasion demanded. *Example*: the lierne vault above the high altar and mural at Christchurch Priory (Hampshire).

A fine Tudor tower with octagonal turrets: St Peter and St Paul, Henley-on-Thames (Oxon)

Early sixteenth-century window in St Peter and St Paul, Henley-on-Thames (Oxon)

Towers

Some show a marked change from the Perpendicular and have octagonal turrets at each corner of the same type used in other buildings, including country mansions.

Complete Churches

St Osyth (Essex). *Notable feature*: its fine brick arcades. Barton-under-Needwood (Staffordshire). It was completed in 1533 in the Perpendicular style, except for the windows, which are unmistakably Tudor.

Sefton (Lancashire). A typical late Perpendicular creation, with a roof of nearly flat pitch.

Interior Arrangement

Design remained traditional, with chancel and nave flanked by aisles.

Sixteenth-century use of the earlier lierne vaulting (modern mural by Hans Feibush) at Priory Church, Christchurch (Hants)

Screens were still carved and erected in the usual place but were made without roods. Instead they displayed the Royal Arms, a reminder of the monarch's new role as 'supreme head' of the Church of England. Ornament often shows the typical Tudor cresting.

Renaissance Influence

The Italian Renaissance, which had paved the way for newer and broader thinking in all the arts, had comparatively little effect upon church architecture of the period; its impact was delayed as a result of the religious controversy engendered by the Reformation.

Among the comparatively few examples of Renaissance work in this period are: the Howard memorials, Framlingham (Suffolk); tombs at Layer Marney (Essex); and at Oxborough (Norfolk, 1520–5); heads of bench ends at Talland (Cornwall); and the octagonal porch of 1562 at Sunninghill (Berkshire), added by John Jewel, Bishop of Salisbury, which is partly Renaissance and partly Perpendicular Gothic in execution.

There are also two works of special merit: the screen and choir stalls of King's College Chapel (Cambridge) – the name of the carver is not known, but the quality of the work is unsurpassed; and the flamboyant vaulting of the de la Warr chantry chapel at Boxgrove Priory (Sussex). The latter shows a strong Italian influence, but most artists and craftsmen who reached England during the sixteenth century were refugees from Flanders and Germany. Here the Renaissance had not been thoroughly assimilated.

6 Stuart (1603-1714)

Background

Under the first two Stuart kings, James I (1603–25) and Charles I (1625–49), renewed religious controversy with increasingly political overtones heralded the *Civil War* (1642–9), followed by republican *Commonwealth* and puritan dictatorship. Not surprisingly, the effects of the later Renaissance upon English church architecture were again delayed, despite a modest start under James I and Charles I. This burst into full life after the *Restoration* of Charles II in 1660, especially when the Great Fire of London in 1666 led to a sudden demand for new church buildings.

Yet the Gothic style did not entirely disappear. The importance of altar and pulpit, and of basic church layout, survived all the religious strife and was reaffirmed in the splendid new churches of the later seventeenth century.

Changing Forms of Worship

The English Reformation had led to the replacement of the altar by a wooden table – called the 'Lord's Table' – placed in the nave. This led to overcrowding in the nave and made the chancel largely redundant. *Archbishop Laud* (1633–40) solved this problem by moving the Lord's Table back to its original position at the east end of the church. He insisted that there were historical reasons for doing this, that in no way did it clash with the spirit of the reformed Church, and that it was necessary in any case to give the priest more room to conduct the Communion service. He also protested that it was disrespectful to have the table in a position where people could and did place their hats on it.

The term 'altar' became common again, despite its changed significance. It was not to be shrouded in mystery, as in the Gothic period, but it was to be a perpetual reminder of Christ's offering to the world and, as such, was worthy of the greatest respect. It was also slightly raised so that the priest could be heard more clearly, and altar

Detail shows superb carving on seventeenth-century pulpit at St Mary,
Stoke d'Abernon (Surrey)

rails were introduced. Now people could come to the altar in relays during Communion instead of remaining in the chancel for most of the service.

The Need for New Design

The role of the priest since the Reformation had been changed. Services were now held in English, and this was partly responsible for the removal of the spiritual barrier between priest and congregation. It was essential that the priest should be clearly heard and seen throughout the church. This meant that existing church buildings were sometimes inadequate. Greater audibility and better vision between nave and chancel were both needed. So, too, was extra seating for the congregation which, in the towns, was increasing in size.

Renaissance-style Churches

Pioneers in Italian Renaissance architecture were initially concerned with the reproduction of Classical forms. Fifteenth-century pioneers were Brunelleschi, Donatello, and Alberti. In the sixteenth century it became a formulated style and was consolidated by the works of Vignola and Palladio.

Now, in seventeenth-century England, there were those who thought that the Classical concept would be suited to religious and secular buildings. It could be used to produce a place of worship that was basically a single room with the required audience–lecturer quality: an *auditory church*. In addition, it could achieve a sense of beauty and proportion, even if it did not aspire, as did the Gothic, to convey a sense of the eternal from soaring arches, vaults and spires.

The Classical Orders

The basis of the new Renaissance church was the free use of the old classical 'orders' which had originated in Greece and had been adopted by the Romans with minor modifications. These are:

Doric – The oldest of the classical orders. The *column* rises upon a circular base on a square *plinth*. It is fluted with channels less than a semi-circle in section and separated from each other by a sharp edge.

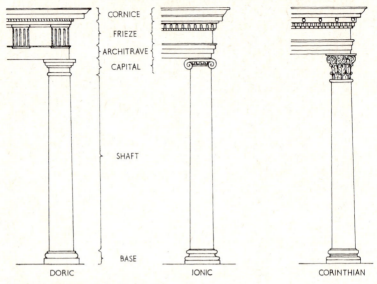

The three orders of classical building

Its plain, moulded *capital* has a square upper section (*abacus*) and is connected with the shaft of the column by an *ovolo*, or quarter-round moulding, with a small neck-mould below.

Ionic – The *column* is fluted with deeper channels, separated from each other by a fillet or flat edge. It stands upon a moulded *base*, and its capital is adorned with a double spiral scroll (*volute*).

Corinthian – Similar to Ionic, but the *capital* is deeper and, while it has some *volutes*, these are fewer and surrounded with foliage or acanthus leaves.

On top of the appropriate columns rests the *entablature* – rectangular or semi-circular – consisting of three parts: *architrave*, *frieze*, and *cornice*. Windows, whether above or below the entablature, are generally round-headed, occasionally rectangular. Above one storey the higher windows, if round-headed, have flatter arches.

The Corinthian order was the most favoured. Elaborate rules, based on the classic formula, were developed for determining the exact proportions for each part of the work.

First Auditory Churches

St Paul, Covent Garden (London). Begun 1630. Architect, Inigo Jones (1573–1652), who also designed the Banqueting Hall, Whitehall. This first Renaissance church to be built in England shows masterly treatment in composition, despite a plain exterior. The eastern face has an open colonnaded porch (*portico*) with a *pediment* – a low-pitched gable of triangular shape – supported by four Tuscan columns. The eaves are deep. Inside, the lofty interior is undivided and aisleless, but contains a three-sided gallery.

St Nicholas, Hulcote (Bedfordshire). The arch between nave and chancel is decorative only, not structural, and the church is basically a single room.

Gothic Survival Churches

Holy Trinity, Wyke Champflower (Somerset). The small rectangular church (a chapelry of Bruton) is attached to the manor house and was rebuilt in 1623 in Jacobean Gothic.

St John, Briggate (Leeds). Completed in 1632, this is one of the last parish churches to be built in 'surviving' Gothic: that is, in Gothic as a living tradition. The masonry is pure Gothic, except for the ornament on pillar caps. Screen, pews and pulpit, with pulpit canopy (*tester*) above, are Jacobean Renaissance work; the triangular sections between arches (*spandrels*) above the screen show the new style in masonic decoration – a flat pierced stonework known as *strapwork*.

Woodcarving and Sculpture

The woodwork of the period is renowned for its boldness; the somewhat rarer monumental carving is also very striking and of the highest quality. *Examples*: the pulpit at St Mary, Stoke D'Abernon (Surrey); the magnificent Lewys memorial at the collegiate church of the Blessed Virgin Mary, Edington (Wiltshire); and the effigy of Alice, Countess of Derby, dated 1636, at St Mary, Harefield (Middlesex).

Gothic and Classical Styles Blended

Some bold experiments were made by groups of architects to combine Gothic and Classical Renaissance styles in one work. The blending produced some incongruity. *Examples*:

St Catherine Creechurch (London). Rebuilt by Laud in a blend of the two styles.

St Mary, Leighton Bromswold (Huntingdonshire). Restored 1632–6. Gothic Perpendicular in window tracery. Jacobean Renaissance furnishings and Renaissance tower.

Holy Trinity and St Mary, Abbey Dore (Herefordshire). Renaissance timberwork of roof and screen designed by John Abel in 1634. The church is early medieval.

In Oxford and Cambridge there are a number of college chapels that show similar blending. *Examples*: the chapels of Oriel and Brasenose, Oxford. At the latter the large east window, looking out on the square of the Radcliffe Camera, has typical Gothic tracery, above which is a classical pediment and surrounding ornament. At Cambridge, Peterhouse chapel (1639) presents the two styles in some confusion, with pilasters – small pillars attached to the wall behind – that are Renaissance in their lower parts but Gothic above.

Sir Christopher Wren

With the Restoration of the Monarchy of 1660 came the full impact of the Renaissance influence upon church architecture under Sir Christopher Wren. Gothic, which continued even then, was now a conscious imitation of the old style, not a development of it.

Wren could work in Gothic if required to do so, but his choice was to follow the Renaissance tradition, using certain modifications or additions. Some of his detail is Greek; his arches are round in the manner of the Romanesque; his domes are eastern.

Wren's great skill was his adaptability, knowing always what was right for a particular purpose, and nowhere is this better shown than in his masterpiece: St Paul's Cathedral. Here he followed the main lines of the old Norman building, combined these with an exterior rich in Classic detail, and produced the effect of a consistent whole. The west towers give dignity and strength to the whole façade, recalling in their main outline the general idea of many a Gothic front.

Wren's earlier parish churches, built while the plans for St Paul's were not finally settled, showed various essays in dome construction. When the cathedral had at last taken shape, the original dome construction was abandoned – it had been experimental.

Undomed churches follow the plan of a simple nave and aisles with recessed sanctuary and flat ceiling, imposing a graceful design on what is basically a rectangular hall. To towers and spires Wren gave special attention, since his purpose in rebuilding the churches of the City after the Great Fire of 1666 was to allow them to make their presence felt. If they could not do this with the mass of secular buildings around them, then at least they should be seen upon the skyline.

Wren's churches show a variety of styles, so that one is barely conscious of any repetition. All reflect the spirit and temperament of their time, with provision for the dignity of the sanctuary and the administration of the sacraments. Great care was always given to the altarpiece, with its details, to the rails which enclosed the altar, and to the screens when these were used. The marble fonts, with their fine covers, show exquisite detail.

Although Wren's architectural work was confined almost exclusively to London, his influence was far reaching and ensured the dominance of classical architecture for more than a century. Succeeding styles, however, even those of his immediate followers, were often developed with a greater degree of variation from the pattern of the early Renaissance.

Examples of Wren City Churches:

St Benet, Paul's Wharf. In Thames Street, among wharves and warehouses; rectangular; graced by a beautiful dome and *lantern* – the name given to a structure surmounting a dome or roof to admit light.

St Bride, Fleet Street. Opened in 1675, the first to be built after the Great Fire. *Main feature*: an elegant spire in diminishing stages like a telescope or a wedding cake; completed in 1703. Restored in 1958 after being gutted in World War II.

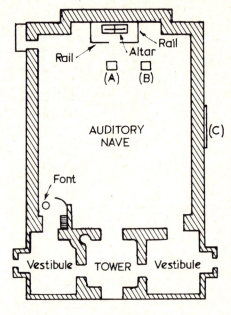

A—Original position of pulpit
B—present position
C—Original side-door,
   excluded on re-building.

Seventeeth-century auditory church (St James, Piccadilly, London)

St Clement Danes. Built by Wren 1680–2, the steeple by his eminent
pupil James Gibbs. Gutted in 1941. *Interior features*: gallery,
curved east end, and vaulted ceiling.

St Clement, Eastcheap. One of Wren's small churches in straight-
forward classical style.

St James, Garlick Hythe. Though plan is Gothic-style, interior is
classical, with much Renaissance woodwork. A noble church, with
a fine tower and steeple of Portland stone.

St James, Piccadilly. Built 1682–4; restored by Sir Albert Richardson
in 1953 after war damage. One of the few churches built by Wren
on an unencumbered site. The aim was to seat two thousand people
who could see the preacher and hear him distinctly. The gallery plan
was an integral part of the building and was adopted for most large
town churches during the next 150 years. *Special feature*: barrel
vaulting carried by columns rising from gallery. Carving on festoon
of reredos and on font by Grinling Gibbons.

The mastery of Sir Christopher Wren: St Mary At Hill, Eastcheap, London

St Lawrence Jewry. Built 1671–7, gutted in World War II, and now
restored. Rectangular plan, severe but dignified. Now the Lord
Mayor's official church.
St Margaret, Lothbury. Worked in Portland stone, with tower and

A classic Wren steeple – St Mary-le-Bow

lead-covered spire. *Interior features*: broad nave, north aisle, and clerestory. Fine pulpit with tester and screen are from All Hallows' the Great.

St Margaret Pattens, Eastcheap. ('Pattens' or wooden sandals were once made in the neighbourhood.) Rebuilt by Wren 1684–7. Its Gothic-type spire is unusual. Contemporary canopied pews, font, and fine carving with a Stuart lion and unicorn.

St Martin, Ludgate. Vaulted ceiling in shape of Greek cross. Delicate spire acts as a foil to the dome of St Paul's when viewed from Fleet Street.

St Mary, Abchurch. Built of brick, with tower and lead spire. Magnificent interior, richly decorated. Square nave and chancel in single unit, above which a dome is supported by a structure of eight concave triangular members (*pendentives*) to form an umbrella-type vault.

St Mary At Hill. The dome is carried by four Doric columns which also form the aisles and give the interior a cruciform appearance. Ceiling takes the shape of a Greek cross. Interior very rich, with original high pews, and attractive wood and ironwork on altarpiece, pulpit, and over west gallery. Some of the woodwork, including the pulpit, is nineteenth century – but in seventeenth-century style – by William Gibbs Rogers.

St Mary-le-Bow. Has a tall tower with Doric doorways and the most elaborate of all the Wren steeples.

St Mary, Somerset. Only the tower remains. This is surrounded by an unusual crop of obelisks and urns some 20ft high.

St Michael, Paternoster Row. One of Wren's later churches, built between 1686–1713. Octagonal but curved steeple similar to that on the western towers of St Paul's. Tower itself is plain.

St Vedast, Foster Lane. Tower has two receding stages in upper section, capped by an attractive small steeple. In near distance can be seen the taller and grander steeple of St Mary-le-Bow. Both churches were begun in 1670.

Outside London a church of Wren's design is St Mary, Ingestre (Staffordshire), built in 1676 – originally as a private chapel – on a square plan. The chancel is paved with black and white marble, and an interesting feature is the Flanders oak screen with the royal arms above.

All Saints, Farley (Wiltshire), completed in 1688, may also be of Wren's design. It still possesses its original contemporary furnishings.

Robert Hooke – an associate of Wren's and a fellow member of the Royal Society – built the church of St Mary Magdalene, Willen (Buckinghamshire). The tower, like that of St Mary, Ingestre, is squat in its lower section, but it has good detail. Inside are the original high pews and font.

7 Georgian and Victorian (1714-1901)

Background

The 'Glorious Revolution' of 1688 which expelled James II had far-reaching effects on the evolution of English churches. The revolution prevented the widely-feared return of Roman Catholicism as the official religion of the country. Both James and his elder brother Charles II had cultivated political and religious ties with Catholic France, a trend which threatened to make this a reality.

Under William III (1689–1702), Anne (1702–14) and the House of Hanover up to 1837 the pendulum swung very much in the opposite direction. The mystery of the altar did not become paramount: it was replaced as a focal point of worship by the increasingly dominant role of the pulpit.

In the eighteenth century religious toleration slowly made ground, and noncomformists – members of Protestant Christian Churches other than the Church of England – were allowed to worship in their own way in separate buildings. But Roman Catholics were still distrusted and freedom for them was considerably delayed. 'Catholic Emancipation' became something of a political football, but English Catholics were prevented from holding political office until 1829.

The nineteenth century saw a spiritual revival within the Church which followed on the heels of the late eighteenth-century 'Romantic movement', noted for its fondness for dramatic Gothic ruins. The best examples of English church building in the eighteenth century still relied on the classical Renaissance, but using a freer form. First attempts were made to revive the Gothic style – but not as a living structure. This is now known as 'Gothick'.

A spiritual revival that began in the early nineteenth century was spearheaded by the so-called 'Oxford Movement' and its eminent advocates Pusey, Newman, and Keble. Hand in hand with this revival came the attempt to build again in Gothic as a structural form. Soon this 'Gothic revival' became the accepted vogue throughout the country, and was carried through to the present century.

New Classical Styles

Baroque

A new style of Renaissance architecture, practised in Italy and known as *baroque*, sought to obtain a more dramatic effect by the greater use of mass and bolder detail. This spread to other parts of Europe, and it was applied in England by Wren's successors. One, Sir John Vanbrugh (1664–1726), designed impressive country mansions, while his contemporary Nicholas Hawksmoor (1661–1736) built several churches. These are inclined to be rather solemn in appearance, but they have considerable merit and are widely admired; the interiors are well planned.

Examples of Hawksmoor churches: St Alfege, Greenwich (1711–14); St Anne, Limehouse (1712–24); St Mary Woolnoth, Lombard Street (1716–27); and Christ Church, Spitalfields (1723–9). All were constructed in Portland stone and built under the provisions of the 1711 Act of Parliament which provided for the erection of fiftyone new churches in the City of London and its immediate suburbs. Like Wren, Hawksmoor worked mainly in London, but he was responsible for the fine great west door of Beverley Minster, with its evangelists and their symbols.

Among other architects who worked in the baroque style were Henry Aldrich (1647–1710), Dean of Christchurch; and Thomas Archer (1668–1743). Aldrich is reputed to have built All Saints, Oxford (1707–8), which is decorated all round by flat Corinthian pilasters broken only by a pedimented porch. Thomas Archer's most mature work is seen in St Philip, Birmingham (now the cathedral), begun in 1709; St Paul, Deptford (begun 1712); and St John, Smith Square, London (1714–28), with four corner towers, and which was restored after being gutted in 1941.

Palladian

In reaction to grand baroque came a counter movement: a retreat to the strictly classical medium as taught by Palladio and practised earlier in England by Inigo Jones and to some extent by Wren. Under the Earl of Burlington's patronage the movement gained strength,

Beverley Minster (Yorks) Gothic church with a classical West Door

though much of its work was secular in nature: for example, the development of eighteenth-century Bath.

James Gibbs (1682–1752) was the chief Palladian exponent in church architecture, but there were occasions when he used a freer idiom. Following a period of study in Italy he built the elegant St Mary-le-Strand, with its two-storey façade, for the 1711 Commission. His most famous church, St Martin-in-the-Fields (1722–6), was widely copied after he published the plan in his *Book of Architecture* in 1728. St Martin's, with its then unusually placed steeple, which rises from the west wall behind the entrance portico, became a standard pattern for larger churches. Corinthian pilasters surround the exterior. Internal columns rising above the galleried pews support the vaulted nave ceiling with its fine plasterwork.

Among similar-style eighteenth century churches are: St Giles-in-the-Fields, London, by Henry Flitcroft; St John, Wolverhampton (Staffordshire), by William Baker; and Holy Cross, Daventry (Northamptonshire), by David Hiorn. Small churches of the period continued to be in the Wren tradition, but plainer. The interiors were

Familiar to millions: the elegant porch and steeple of St Martin-in-the-Fields, Trafalgar Square, London

chiefly taken up by the nave, though sometimes there were aisles. Chancels were short. The presence of a tower would distinguish such a building from a nonconformist chapel.

Changing Older Churches

To cope with increasing congregations Georgian architects worked to a simple plan – they added galleries to many of the older churches, and this sometimes had the added benefit of improving the auditory effect. St Thomas, Lymington (Hampshire), is a good example of a moderate sized medieval church with eighteenth-century galleries added; the interior is shown in the photograph below.

The Pulpit

The Elizabethan settlement had allowed for the provision of a reading pew in the chancel, after which custom had led to the placing of a desk in the nave – the forerunner of a special litany desk. But as most church interiors were having to cope with larger congregations, and space was short, it seemed logical to group these two positions together, and finally to link them with the pulpit.

The result was a pulpit of novel design, comprising either one or

Eighteenth-century galleries in a medieval church: St Thomas, Lymington (Hants)

two storeys. The lower or lowest storey provided a desk with a diminutive seat for the parish clerk, who took part in the service and read the first lesson and the Epistle from the sitting position. In the case of the three-storey pulpit, the middle stage was used by the priest for reading the second lesson and the Gospel, while the top storey was the position for reading the sermon – a lengthy affair in those days. The sermon came at the end of the service and was read from a prepared text.

There were historical precedents in ancient Christian worship for placing the pulpit in a central position, or for an alternative arrangement where two pulpits or twin desks (or one pulpit and one desk) known as *ambos* were placed at either side of the nave. In fact, the central position was now favoured for acoustic reasons, but the increasing importance of the pulpit as a 'liturgical centre' served to diminish the significance of the altar as the principal focus of worship.

Much of the morning service was conducted from the pulpit during the Georgian period. The separate Holy Communion service was still rare, because the Prayer Book ordered that the Sacrament should not be administered unless several people had given notice that they were willing to partake of it – and few did give notice. Therefore, except on the occasional 'Sacrament Sunday', the Communion service, known in this context as 'Ante-Communion', was combined with Morning Prayer and the Litany, and the whole service lasted about two hours.

The amount of care and attention lavished upon the pulpit is exemplified in the beautiful carving that one finds on a Georgian 'two-decker' or 'three-decker'. Some were provided with music stands, because in small rural communities where there was no choir or organ the priest led the singing. Other special fixtures were for wigs or for hourglasses used in timing the sermon. Sounding boards (*testers*) or canopies were usual.

Other Georgian Fittings

Altars and Surrounds
Altars were made either of stone or of wood – the choice of material

was no longer significant. Space was allowed for surrounding rails on three sides to allow greater room for communicants. Classical surrounds were made up of suitable pillars crowned by the usual pediment. Within this area the function of the medieval reredos is taken up by paintings, or, in less wealthy parishes, by plaques containing the Creed, the Lord's Prayer, and the Ten Commandments. The altar was kept free from unnecessary ornaments.

Bequest Boards

Rectangular boards attached to the front of the gallery to acknowledge gifts of various kinds from benefactors. These included items donated for the poor of the parish, for the improvement of schools or local housing, for the upkeep of the church fabric, or for the provision of new church fittings.

Cartouche Tablets

These are relatively uncommon and comprise ornate frames attached to a wall, generally enclosing an inscription. Walls were normally limewashed white.

Christening Pews

The font was not always kept in the normal position near to the entrance of the church. Sometimes it was placed by the altar rails, at other times beside the pulpit or within the confines of a special christening pew. This was square in shape, for the use of parents, godparents, and near relatives. *Examples*: Whitchurch, Little Stanmore (Middlesex); Chislehampton (Oxfordshire); King's Norton (Leicestershire).

Funeral Hatchments

Lozenge-shaped canvas frames bearing appropriate blazons and other heraldic devices. These were placed outside the houses of important families when one of their members died, and then, after an interval, they were hung in the parish church. Solid black shading on the left indicated death of a husband, on the right, of a wife. Black shading all round designated an unmarried person, widow or widower.

Hatpegs

Original hatpegs for members of the congregation may still be seen on some nave walls.

Lighting

Churches still lacked any form of bright lighting and relied on candles. The *candelabra* of the period are elegant and often ornate.

Monuments

Their use continued. They were generally coloured, self-confident, and finely executed.

Organ Lofts

The position for the singers and musicians, and for the organ if one existed, was in a gallery on the west side of the church.

Painted Texts

Boldy painted on to walls. Georgian ones are coloured red and employ Roman style lettering; earlier Elizabethan texts are in black.

Seating

Interiors, often lacking in colour owing to the limewashing of walls, presented a feast of rich woodwork. The high, virtually draughtproof box pews, with their baize panelling, separate doors, and, here and there, a finely turned canopy, looked up to the gallery or galleries above.

On the ground floor the pews within the nave were neatly divided, some of them reserved for rate-paying parishioners. At Minstead (Hampshire), there is a squire's pew which is recessed into a transept, provides ample space for retainers, and also gives a comfortable homely touch with its special fireplace.

Late Eighteenth-century Churches

For a time the Palladian style remained popular. Some churches were fitted with very expensive decor and interior work, but always depending upon the wealth of individual patrons. Among the richest

Georgian dignity: the tower and entrance portico of St Peter and St Paul, Blandford (Dorset)

interiors were those created by the Adam brothers. Robert Adam, with his brothers, James, John and William, had built the part of London known as the Adelphi, and an example of a church built by Robert Adam is St Andrew, Gunton (Norfolk), 1769. The exterior is Palladian; the interior is impeccably furnished as a college chapel. St Bartholomew, Binley (Warwickshire), completed in 1773, with its fine interior plasterwork, is also believed to be the work of this architect. Another Adam-style showpiece, but without its contemporary furnishings, is St Peter and St Leonard, Horbury (West Yorkshire), built by John Carr in 1791. It is unusual in that it has apses at both east and west ends. The interior has fluted Corinthian arcades; Ionic columns have been used for the porch.

Towards the end of the century architects were experimenting with the shape of churches, often to good effect. For example, elliptical and round naves were found to be more economical with seating. The round galleries (*rotundas*) were still popular at the beginning of the next century. With rotundas and side galleries members of a congregation would sit facing each other: it was an arrangement that seemed natural to the Georgians. Galleries had in any case been a feature of the Christian Church for many years above the rood and, in the case of certain larger buildings, in the triforium.

Examples of eighteenth-century rotundas:

St Chad, Shrewsbury (Shropshire). Built by George Stewart between 1790–1802. Plan comprises two intersecting circles, the larger forming the auditorium and the smaller forming the entrance hall. Beautiful Adamesque ceiling.

All Saints, Newcastle (Northumberland). Elliptical – almost round – design by David Stephenson, 1786–96. Altar in apsidal recess. Contemporary mahogany pews.

The Greek Influence

The neo-Greek movement began in the eighteenth century and continued into the next; it was powerful in secular as well as in religious architecture.

Examples of classical Greek churches:

All Saints, Nuneham Courtenay (Oxfordshire), begun in 1764, by James Stuart (1713–88), with two porticos.

New Church, Ayot St Lawrence (Hertfordshire), by Nicholas Revett (*c.* 1721–1804). Externally Greek; inside details Roman.

St Pancras New Church, London, by W. and H. W. Inwood. This boldly reproduces the porch of the Athenian Erectheum.

All Souls, Langham Place, London. Built 1822-4 by the celebrated architect John Nash, to whom goes the credit for the fine buildings of Regent Street.

Georgian 'Gothick'

Gothic-style buildings – known at this period as 'Gothick' – were still appearing in eighteenth-century religious and secular architecture. They were less numerous than the classical designs and expressed a movement towards romanticism. It was rare for Gothic to be built now as a living structure, but it could achieve pleasing results at times.

Examples of Georgian Gothick churches:

Blessed Virgin Mary, Preston-on-Stour (Warwickshire). Rebuilt in 1752 in Gothick. The contemporary glass is melancholic in theme.

St John the Evangelist, Shobdon (Herefordshire). Originally Norman; rebuilt in 1753 in extravagant or 'rococo' Gothick. Outsize pews, painted white; much ornament and bright colour.

St Mary Magdalene, Croome (Worcestershire), 1763. Gothick throughout.

All Saints, Hindley (Lancashire), 1766. Classical round-headed windows have Gothick tracery. Black and gold interior gallery.

St Andrew, Boynton (East Yorkshire). Medieval, rebuilt in brick in 1768 with Gothick details in classical structure, including imitation plaster vault in tower.

St Mary, Tetbury (Gloucestershire). Built in 1781 by Francis Hiorn, and considered to be a very fine example. Perpendicular style windows; columns thinner than normal Gothic; fake vaulting.

St Mary Magdalene, Stapleford (Leicestershire). Rebuilt in 1783 in Gothick. Interior seats face inwards.

St James, Papplewick (Nottinghamshire). Said to be one of England's finest examples and built in 1795 against a fourteenth-century tower. Porch is same height as nave. Very unusual and varied interior.

St George, Hulme, Manchester (Lancashire). A late example, 1826–7, by Francis Goodwin. Galleried interior. Narrow but heavily pinnacled tower.

Commissioners Churches

The 'Napoleonic' Wars of 1793–1815 severely curtailed churchbuilding. Following the end of hostilities the 1818 Church Building Act allowed one million pounds for the building of new churches in populous districts, including London. A further grant was made in 1824. Of the 214 churches – known as 'Commissioners churches' – built under the Act the majority were in nineteenth-century Gothick with auditory-type interiors. The choice of style was dictated by cost, for bricks, which were more suited to Gothic than to classical work, were relatively cheap; in addition the metal used in pillar and window construction could be produced more readily in the former style.

The early nineteenth-century Commissioners churches have been the subject of much debate concerning their merit or lack of it. Most observers consider them to be rather uninspired.

The Gothic Revival

Victorian Gothic churches are described as 'Gothic Revival' or 'neo-Gothic'. The word Gothic is now spelled without the final 'k', since the style is no longer an imitation of the medieval without its structural features. It began soon after the launching of the new 'Tractarian' or 'Oxford' movement, under John Keble, J. H. Newman and E. B. Pusey, and the declared aim of this movement was to re-establish the Church of England as a reformed member of the Catholic communion. In a famous sermon at Oxford, Keble advanced the principle that the Church needed to regain its spirituality through the application of Catholic doctrine.

The drive for the new architectural style of the period came from a talented draughtsman, A. W. N. Pugin, whose life was becoming increasingly devoted to the study of Gothic art and buildings. He contended that because Catholic ritual was practised in Gothic churches of the medieval period, then Gothic was not only the best but also the only true form for a Christian church to take.

This was illogical, but there were many who championed Pugin's cause. It was not long before research was carried out by 'ecclesiologists' into the sacramental meaning of every part of a church – its appointments and fittings, its background, the manner in which services were conducted in the past, and, in particular, the application of ritual, music, vestments and symbolism. Soon there was a determined drive to build new much-needed churches for the expanding population in 'true Gothic principles' and to convert existing ones to conform to the new dictum.

'Restorations'

It is not to be denied that many older churches were in need of repair at the time, but though some were restored sympathetically, a greater number were subjected to needless structural changes. Plaster was scraped off walls (which was contrary to all previous Gothic practice), and with the plaster went countless beautiful paintings concealed by successive coats of limewash. Medieval glass was removed to make way for contemporary Victorian designs or plain glass, and many objects of beauty such as Renaissance altar rails, galleries, pulpits and pews, monuments and other fittings were ruthlessly destroyed.

The New Plan

When looking at a Victorian church, it will be seen that the earlier sections of this book dealing with the medieval Gothic period broadly apply. Nevertheless, there are certain differences owing to the fact that it was not the intention to return to the pre-Reformation situation in its entirety; this would not have been possible in any case.

New churches after about 1840 generally allowed for a modest-sized chancel with a fairly low roof. This compromised between the long chancel of the large medieval churches and the diminutive one of Renaissance and subsequent auditory buildings. The priest was given a new position, at the west end of the chancel, for while it was

Victorian originality: the chancel of All Saints, Margaret Street, London, by William Butterfield

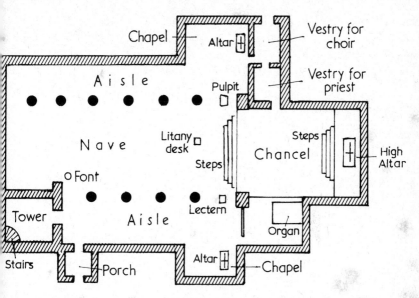

A typical Victorian church: based on the correct 'ecclesiological' principles. Chancel and altar are both raised to stress the altar as the focal point of worship

not desired that he should become remote from the congregation in the proximity of the altar, as at most times during the old service of Mass, neither was it fitting that he should spend too much time in the pulpit, which placed him virtually in the middle of the congregation and made him similar in that respect to a noncomformist minister. As a result of this change his status was thus enhanced, compared to eighteenth-century standards, for while he remained the visible father of his flock and could still be clearly heard, yet by dwelling within the more sacred confines of the building for much of the service, his priestly role as mediator between God and man was emphasised for the first time since the Reformation.

The pulpit was to be, as in medieval times, in the nave to the immediate north-east of the chancel – never centrally placed so as to obstruct the altar.

Seating was made to face east and constructed as low as possible so as to ensure maximum visibility in this direction.

Fonts that had been placed in the body of the nave, or near to the altar rails or pulpit, were replaced in their original position near to the entrance: that is, at the point where one first enters the Church of Christ after baptism.

The choir was no longer to be accommodated in a gallery, but in the lower part of the chancel. Here its members, who were surpliced for the first time, would be in the best position to lead the singing without causing possible distraction to the congregation.

Another objection to the gallery structure was that it caused worshippers who used it to face each other instead of allowing all to see towards the altar as the focal point of worship.

Finally, the Laudian concept of railing off the altar was extended to include the whole of the easternmost part of the chancel known as the sanctuary. This was thus reserved solely for the priest and his assistants, and here could be seen once more the provisions of Catholic worship: the altar candles, the pyx for the reservation of the Sacrament, and, of course, the altar itself with the traditional backing of a reredos. The latter could be carved and gilded, or painted.

The new movement with its accent on Catholic worship came as a challenge not only to church designers, but also to artists, glaziers and other craftsmen. The Church returned to its original role as a great patron of the arts. In addition, many new hymns were written, the psalms were repointed, and the standard of singing improved.

As was to be expected, changes did not proceed at a uniform pace throughout the country, nor were they always welcomed. The previous rather small 'high church' party, known familiarly as 'high and dry', thought that the new form of worship smacked of 'Popery', and to the old 'low church' tradition it was virtually unthinkable. The fact that Newman, one of the founders of the Tractarian movement, together with the architect Pugin 'went over to Rome' did not help matters. Nevertheless, the movement continued to gain strength and is the predominant influence in worship today.

Gothic Revival Churches and their Architects

Many Victorian churches of the period show obvious signs of hurried mass production. These, however, are the imitative products of the lesser architects. There were, at the top, a number of great men such as William Butterfield, G. F. Bodley and J. L. Pearson, whose creative work in the Gothic medium was outstanding.

The following section attempts to describe the styles and objectives of some of the better known architects and give examples of their work. The terms 'Early Pointed', 'Middle Pointed', and 'Late Pointed', used here, and which were current at the time, refer to the arch and window styles of the three respective Gothic periods: Early English, Decorated, and Perpendicular. Some Victorian architects worked in the neo-Norman idiom.

A. W. N. Pugin, 1812–52. Convinced that Gothic was the only true Christian form of architecture. Used Middle Pointed.
  Examples:
  St Laurence, Tubney (Berkshire); and All Saints, Church Leigh (Staffordshire).

Benjamin Ferrey, 1810–80. Built many churches, mostly good Gothic copies and paid much attention to carving.
  Examples:
  St Stephen, Rochester Row, Westminster, 1845–7. Middle Pointed. Lofty, ornate; fine open timber roof.
  St James, Morpeth (Northumberland), 1843–6. Neo-Norman.
  St Michael and All Angels, Chetwynd (Shropshire), 1865–7.
  St Swithin, Wickham (Berkshire), 1854–9. A rebuilt church; tower is eleventh century. Much carving, with angels in nave roof and life-size heads of elephants in north aisle roof.

R. C. Carpenter, 1812–55. Built well-proportioned churches with good mass, detail, and colour.
  Examples:
  St Paul, Brighton (Sussex), 1846–8. Tower lantern by R. H. Carpenter.
  St Mary Magdalene, Munster Square, London, 1849–52. A very beautiful church with chancel designed exactly to the new requirements.

Sir George Gilbert Scott, 1811–78. Most prolific architect of Gothic Revival. Built large churches without screens, generally in Middle Pointed. Liked central tower position for its dramatic interior lighting effect. His restorations were often drastic.

Examples:

Holy Trinity, Halstead (Essex). Towering broach spire. Early Pointed.

All Saints, Ryde (Isle of Wight), 1870. Tall spire.

St John the Baptist, Eastnor (Herefordshire), 1852. Well-proportioned and richly decorated; built on to medieval tower.

St Peter, Croydon (Surrey), 1851. Attractive Middle Pointed church.

St George, Doncaster (West Yorkshire), 1854. Large; cruciform.

William Butterfield, 1814–1900. Used high chancel arches to emphasise most important part of the church. Middle Pointed style adapted with great originality. Obtained texture and contrast from arrangement of coloured bricks in bands or diaper patterns. This was known as 'polychromatic' work.

Examples:

All Saints, Babbacombe, Torquay (Devon), 1868–74. Broad proportions; typical surface texture and ornament; unusual chancel.

All Saints, Margaret Street, London, 1850–9. A skilful design on a small site. Lofty proportions, and most impressive.

St Mary Magdalene, West Lavington (Sussex), 1850. A small sandstone church with materials well suited to rural location. Shingled spirelet.

St James, Baldersby (North Yorkshire), 1857 – with adjacent school and cottages by same architect.

G. E. Street, 1824–81. His design for the London Law Courts had won wide approval. Favoured a single altar (as did Butterfield) that could be clearly seen, and broad, well-lit naves. He built vicarages and schools as well. His restorations were often drastic.

Examples:

St Mary the Virgin, Fawley (Berkshire), 1865–6. Prominent altarpiece under vaulted apse.

All Saints, Brightwalton (Berkshire), 1863. Nave height emphasised by broad low columns, which have large carved capitals.

St John, Torquay (Devon), 1861–71. Spacious church, with wide chancel and high arch. Fine ornament and glass.

St James-the-less, Westminster, 1858–61. Original design, with detached tower. Red granite columns; carved capitals.

St Philip and St James (Oxford), 1860–6. Cruciform. Tapering nave arcades to emphasise length.

All Saints, Denstone (Staffordshire), 1862. Bold design. Ironwork, brass and marble used for interior.

J. L. Pearson, 1817–98. A great architect. For some years he used the French Gothic style, and some of his churches are like small cathedrals with their soaring vaults and fine apses. His greatest work is the cathedral church of Truro.

Examples:

St Mary, Truro (Cornwall) – the Cathedral church. Pearson's design of 1880 incorporates the early sixteenth-century parish church on this site. Early Gothic influence in both the English and French idiom; three towers and central steeple.

St Matthew, Landscove (Devon), 1849–50. Broach spire at east end of south aisle.

St Stephen, Bournemouth (Hampshire), 1881–98. A superb example.

St Agnes, Sefton Park, Liverpool (Lancashire), 1883. Vaulted. Early Pointed; lancet windows.

St Peter, Vauxhall, London, 1863–5. Beautiful, in French style.

St Augustine, Kilburn, London, 1870–80. Largest of Pearson's London churches; double aisles; three-bayed chancel. Triforium extends round whole of building.

St Michael and All Angels, Croydon (Surrey), 1880–5. French Gothic.

St Michael, Headingley (West Yorkshire), 1884–7. Tall spire.

G. F. Bodley, 1827–1907. Believed that nineteenth-century Gothic was a style in its own right. He disagreed with ecclesiologists who contended that original Gothic reached its peak during the early Decorated period, and based his designs – particularly windows – on later styles. These are a blend of Middle and Late Pointed but also show the architect's great originality. He did not favour chancel arches, but preferred screens.

Examples:

All Souls, Leicester, 1907. Lofty, well-lit; pastel colouring.

Holy Trinity, Kensington Gore, London, 1902. A fine example of Bodley's style.

St Michael, Camden Town, London, 1876–81. Grand but restrained.

All Saints, Weston-super-Mare (Avon), 1898–1902. Wagon roof.

St Chad, Burton-on-Trent (Staffordshire), 1910. A low-vaulted passage joins church with tower. Bodley's last church.

Church of the Holy Angels, Hoar Cross (Staffordshire), 1876. Built in the style of an early Gothic cathedral.

Later Work of the Gothic Revival

Other fine exponents of the movement include the two sons of Sir George Gilbert Scott (George Gilbert Scott, Junior, and John Oldrid Scott); Austin and Paley who, in partnership, built many fine churches, including St George, Stockport (Cheshire), 1893–7, with its splendid nave and arcades; and the equally renowned partnership of Clarke and Micklethwaite, who built St Martin, Brighton, 1875.

An architect who, like Pearson, was strongly influenced by Continental Gothic, was William Burges. One of his best known churches is Christ the Consoler, Skelton (West Yorkshire). Sir William Emerson, a pupil of Burges, specialised in the French Gothic style.

Not all Victorian architects conformed precisely to ecclesiological rules. After Bodley's churches had encompassed Late Pointed to some extent there arose a definite later movement to establish the neo-Perpendicular vogue. One exponent, R. R. Johnson, built some impressive churches, including St Matthew, Newcastle (Northumberland), and St Aidan, Leeds (West Yorkshire), well known for its beautiful interior.

While it became acceptable for styles to become increasingly

Victorian sedilia in the Early English style, St Peter and St Paul, Shiplake (Oxon)

ornate, as, for example, with men like Bodley or Henry Woodyer, it was alleged that some of the later architects ignored the essentials of good constructional practice. Bassett Keeling, E. B. Lamb, and S. S. Teulon were criticised for using such devices as cast-iron columns with wrought-iron capitals and a far too brilliant polychromy. The garish effects were not always appreciated, yet one must allow for changing tastes and later judgements. Sir Arthur Blomfield, whose work extended nearly to the twentieth century, and who built fine churches in a variety of styles, declared that he was actually in favour of cast-iron columns, since these were less of a hindrance to visibility than the normal ones built of stone.

One attempt to break away from conventional building styles, and which attracted much support, was the so-called 'Arts and Craft' movement. This had its roots in the work of the pre-Raphaelite painters, Burne-Jones, William Morris, Rossetti, and Maddox Brown, who had designed stained glass and received commissions from Street, Pearson, and others. In the course of time the movement became identified with a free style of building based on Late Pointed but that was free of restriction in the use of materials and the manner of decoration.

A superb example of an Arts and Craft church is J. D. Sedding's Holy Trinity, Sloane Street, London (1888–90), with its impressive 'Perpendicular' front and 'Tudor' octagonal towers. In another design, that of St Peter, Mount Park Road, Ealing, Sedding's great west window is trisected by buttresses – a device that was widely used by W. D. Caröe and some other architects of the period. A different style is seen in The Holy Redeemer, Clerkenwell, London, which is again the work of Sedding. The Italian-type campanile tower was designed by his pupil, H. Wilson. The interior of this remarkable church is dominated by Sedding's Renaissance-inspired altar-piece in the manner of Wren.

It should be noted that Victorian churches were never meant to be taken for medieval, although they have often been criticised for failing to pass as such. There is no doubt that today their merits are becoming more widely appreciated.

8 The Twentieth Century

Background

There were no marked changes in the manner of Anglican worship or changes in the basic style of church-building in the immediate post-Victorian period. New churches of the commodious nineteenth-century type were built as required – mainly in suburbs of large towns and in growing seaside resorts – to cope with the spiritual requirements of the expanding population.

Great social changes occasioned by two world wars led to changes in the Church's ministry. Together, these meant that the design of new church buildings would need to depart from previous concepts.

The period between the two wars, but more particularly the years following World War II, have seen much experiment in religious architecture. With soaring costs the ever-present need to use materials and labour as economically as possible has presented church architects with a great challenge.

The Last Gothic Churches

At the beginning of the twentieth century it was still an economical proposition to build in the Gothic style, and no one challenged it – there was no need to do so. Large congregations in expanding towns and seaside resorts needed large churches, so that when new ones were built the previous architectural concepts needed little or no modification. What is more, the eminent builders of the age were all well versed in the old Gothic tradition. Among them, to name just some, were Sir Walter Tapper, G. H. Fellowes-Prynne, Temple Moore, Sir Charles Nicholson, Sir Giles Gilbert Scott (grandson of Sir George Gilbert Scott, and who, at the age of twenty-one, submitted the winning design for the new Liverpool Cathedral), Sir Edward Maufe, architect of Guildford Cathedral, and Sir J. Ninian Comper.

Comper, who died in 1960 at the age of 94, was an accomplished architect, as well as being a gifted designer and restorer of church

Elegant arcade in the Early English style at St Wilfrid, Harrogate (Yorks) by Temple Moore – completed in 1935

fittings. In his early career he worked for Bodley, and in all his buildings, from his original neo-Perpendicular to his later freer style, he aimed to fulfil one constant objective: this he called 'beauty by inclusion', by which criterion a church is judged solely by whether or not it 'succeeds in eliminating time and producing the atmosphere of heavenly worship'. Certainly this was the case with Comper's own work where Gothic and Renaissance styles generally blend well in the

Spire of John Keble Church, Mill Hill, London, by D. F. Martin-Smith (1938)

interior decor – as, for example, in the great vaulted church of St Mary, Wellingborough, Northamptonshire, consecrated in 1908 but not completed until 1931.

New Concepts

Today there is no standard form of architecture that appears to be distinctly 'religious' or suitable for the needs of an Anglican church.

One reason is that the contrasts between the urban and rural parts of the ministry are wider than they ever were before, and, in many cases the various considerations involved mean that each new building has to be an experiment in itself.

Certainly, it would no longer be economically possible to build structurally in the Gothic tradition, even if this is what everyone wanted. At this point we face conflicting problems, because if all are agreed that to continue to give 'Gothic touches' to new churches is out of place, then do we still want our churches as we build them to have Comper's 'atmosphere of heavenly worship'? In which case, what else can one do to create such an atmosphere? The stained glass window, the pillared aisle, the pointed arch over door or window – these are really all vestiges of a medieval tradition that is now passed.

On the other hand, can we say that the rejection of what appear to be false notes of romanticism has produced a better type of building? Inevitably, unless very special care is taken, the construction nowadays of a large town church or a hybrid church and social centre results in a building that seems every bit as secular as a theatre or a police station. The surmounting cross may be the only evidence from the exterior that this is not a civil establishment of some kind.

Why this happens is a matter which, if debated, could assist patrons and architects in the future. It must be conceded that, with large buildings, the use of structural materials is determined by their cost and availability, but why is it that interiors tend to be so bare? Renaissance builders needed plain auditory-type interiors, but, to some extent like Comper in our own century, they aimed at 'beauty by inclusion' and nearly always succeeded.

To many, therefore, the challenge of the present century has not yet been met. Perhaps we are still very undecided as to what a church should really present in the architectural and decorative forms. We can argue that money spent on a place for Christians to worship, should now be kept strictly to a minimum. On the other hand we may decide that to build a beautiful – even a relatively costly – church is a laudable rather than culpable objective.

Future church design will depend to a great extent on which of these two views will prevail or if a compromise is possible.

St Sidwell, Exeter (Devon), completed in 1957 on the site of the church
destroyed in World War II

A Final Walk round the Church and a Look at the Churchyard

Altar Coverings

The medieval arrangement is described on p 64. Today the coverings comprise the *frontal* of woven fabric; a *frontlet*, which is in effect a pelmet attached to an undercloth on top of the altar; and a 'fair linen cloth', as mentioned in the Reformation Prayer Book, which covers the undercloth, extends across the whole of the altar top and may hang down slightly at either end.

The 'fair linen cloth' is always white. The others are made in the liturgical colours that have been observed by long custom in Anglican churches – namely, white for joy, purity or triumph, as at Christmas, Easter, Ascensiontide, Trinity, and on feast days of the Virgin Mary, angels, and saints (excluding martyrs); red for fire, as at Whitsun and on martyrs' feast days; purple for penitence, as during Advent, Lent, and on the three Sundays preceding Lent; and black or a neutral colour for mourning, as on Good Friday. Green, as the colour of the countryside, stands for life and hope and is used at other times.

Altar Vessels

These are used during the service of Holy Communion or Parish Communion; otherwise they are locked for safe keeping. They comprise the cup (*chalice*) for the wine; circular plate (*paten*) for wafers (bread is rarely used); *cruets* or *flagons* for the wine and the water; and a small box for unconsecrated wafers. Very few medieval vessels remain. High churches use additional vessels for incense and holy oils. The *pyx* suspended above the altar is now the customary vessel in high churches for the reservation of the Sacrament: alternatively, a special wall cupboard (*aumbry*) is used, as in former centuries.

Candles

Altar candles are generally known as 'lights'. By tradition, two candles only should be used; some high churches use six.

Cross and Crucifix

In former times the upper part of the *processional cross* was detached and placed upon the altar during the service. Now an altar will have its own *cross* or *crucifix*, placed centrally.

Flowers

The use of altar vases for flowers is comparatively recent. Flowers are normally placed in the region around the pulpit and in front of the lectern – and, at flower or harvest festival times, all round the church. The Harvest Festival service dates from the last century and was begun by Robert Stephen Hawker, the poet vicar of Morwenstow (Cornwall).

Lighting

Chandeliers, where they exist, are wired for mains electricity. Some modern lighting and heating systems appear out of keeping when units are suspended from piers of nave arcades. Nineteenth-century oil lanterns, now electrified, are still occasionally seen.

Stations of the Cross

The display of paintings or carvings placed around the walls of a church, depicting scenes of Our Lord's Passion. This is a long accepted tradition for Roman Catholic but not for Anglican churches.

Staves

These are attached to pews on either side of the nave where the two churchwardens sit. On top of each stave is an emblem connected with the church. The use of staves dates from the sixteenth century. (*See* 'Stave Lockers', p 72.)

Outside the Church

Leaving via the porch, as one entered, there are various notices relating to church and parish events, and details of any special appeals. Outside the porch there may be a *sundial*, probably eighteenth or nineteenth century in origin, or possibly a medieval *scratchdial*. There are still a number of these to be seen, and they were used to mark the times at which services were held before clocks were invented.

Wall scratchings known as *graffiti* are occasionally seen. For example, at Awliscombe, near Honiton (Devon), there is the incised outline of a woman's hand, with the date 1708, known as the 'bride's hand' and probably connected with an old fertility rite. Other wall incisions include *masons' marks*, *pilgrims' crosses*, and *consecration crosses* – as already described on p 73.

In olden days fugitives could claim the right of sanctuary by clasping the ring of the *sanctuary knocker* on the porch door, though, according to law, he was safe for forty days upon reaching the consecrated ground of the churchyard. The right of sanctuary was abolished in 1623.

Churchyards are sometimes described as 'God's Acre', because they have been consecrated by a bishop. Some churchyards contain *ancient crosses* dating from the times of earliest Christianity (*see* p 16) but, more frequently, a *cross on a plinth of several steps* that was erected during the Middle Ages to warn the traveller that he was approaching hallowed ground. It also served as a place for open air preaching. Many of these crosses were damaged after the Reformation or during the Civil War or Commonwealth periods.

Epitaphs in churchyards form an interesting part of our social history, and allowances may be made for excesses of wit, or even for libel. Some *tombs* are very old; these are usually in table form. *Yew trees* were popular in a churchyard, partly because of their slow growth, but also on account of their poisonous leaves which meant that farmers were not tempted to graze their cattle in the immediate vicinity.

Many *lychgates* were built during the nineteenth century; there are also a few surviving older ones. They were generally constructed of timber, under a thatched roof giving protection to the flat board or table beneath. This was a convenient place for the coffin to be placed, where the bearers could await the priest.

Weathervanes attached to church towers are traditional and may take the form of a cock – symbolising St Peter's three denials of Jesus – or perhaps the emblem of a patron saint. Other emblems are usually fishes, dragons, or ships.

Clocks are also common on church towers. Up to the seventeenth century there were no mechanical clocks in general use throughout the parishes of England. Some of the older ones, known as *'Jack' clocks*, comprise figures that boldly strike out at the quarters or the hours. *Example*: the clock known locally as 'Matthew the Miller and his two sons' at St Mary Steps, Exeter (Devon). On some old clocks there are letters instead of numbers. These present miniature texts such as 'Watch and Pray' and 'Glory be to God'.

Reminding one of the days when people came to church on horseback are the *mounting blocks* or *pieces of chain* that may sometimes be found secured to church walls; the latter could also be used for tying up cattle if the drovers were attending a service. Some country parishes provided stabling for horses.

Stocks, pillories, and *ducking stools* are parish mementos still preserved by a few churches. At Alwington (Devon), the old village stocks have been kept, somewhat inappropriately, next to the font. Some parishes still retain their old *church house*, formerly the social centre where ales were brewed and travellers accommodated. *Tithe barns* are also still to be seen. Many are very ancient and stored the produce paid to the priest as part of his dues from the parish under the tithe provisions.

Further Reading

Anderson, M.D. *Looking for History in British Churches*, John Murray, 1951

Betjeman, Sir John (Editor) *Collins Guide to English Parish Churches*, 1958

Clarke, Basil F.L. *Church Builders of the Nineteenth Century*, SPCK, 1938, New Edition, David & Charles, 1969

Clarke, Basil and Betjamin, Sir John *English Churches*, Studio Vista, 1964

Cox, J.C. and Ford, C.B. *The Parish Churches of England*, Batsford, 1935

Delderfield, E.R. *Church Furniture*, David & Charles, 1966

Fisher, E.A. *Saxon Churches of Sussex*, David & Charles, 1970

Jones, Lawrence E. *The Observer's Book of Old English Churches*, Warne, 1969

Slader, J.M. *The Churches of Devon*, David & Charles, 1968

Smith, J.C.D. *Church Woodcarvings – A Westcountry Study*, David & Charles, 1969

Wickham, A.K. *Churches of Somerset*, David & Charles, 1965

Acknowledgements

For permission to reproduce photographs I wish to thank Robin Clifford, Grosvenor Crescent Mews, London; Rector of St Mary-le-Bow, Cheapside, London; and Mr J. D. Simson, Beverley, Yorks. The staff of All Saints, Margaret Street, London, kindly supplied photographs and information.

In addition, thanks for assistance in the selection of photographs is due to Mr C. Farthing and the staff of the National Monuments Record; and to the following I owe thanks for information given: Mr Peter A. T. Burman of the Council for Places of Worship; the Secretary of the Historic Churches Preservation Trust; and Mr Ivor Bulmer-Thomas, Honorary Director of the Friends of Friendless Churches.

Index

David & Charles have a book on it

A Guide to Church Woodcarvings by J. C. D. Smith. The beautiful church woodcarvings of the Middle Ages, which can be seen on bench-ends in even the smallest and remotest of village churches, are an unending source of interest. Here the subjects of the carvings and their meanings are explained, and over 100 superb photographs have been selected from the author's vast collection to illustrate the humour and fun, the sports and games, the popular stories and travellers' tales, the saints, devils, animals, birds, trades and scenes of everyday life which inspired the medieval carvers. Illustrated.

Priories and Abbeys of England by Garry Hogg. Some two or three hundred monastic establishments, founded around the time of the Norman Conquest, are to be found in England. Though few of the buildings remain intact, their beautiful ruins are well worth the time and effort involved in visiting them. For this book the author has selected fifty examples throughout the country, and with a magnificent photograph and brief facing text describes the history, architecture and present state of each. Illustrated.

The Saxon Churches of Sussex by E. A. Fisher. A comprehensive architectural and historical study of all the Saxon churches for which the county of Sussex is famous. After outlining the historical, geological and geographical aspects of the background against which the churches developed, the book proceeds to detailed descriptions of sixty churches. Illustrated.